This workbook was created by and is copyright © 2014 Luther M. Maddy III

All rights are retained by the author of this material.

Reproduction of any part of this material is prohibited without the written permission of the author. The author makes no claims either expressed or implied as to the correctness or suitability of this material.

Microsoft®, Word®, Excel®, Outlook®, and PowerPoint® are registered trademarks of Microsoft Corporation.

Conventions used:

    Keys to be pressed are enclosed in parenthesis such as: press (Enter).

    Text to be typed, when included in an exercise step will be shaded. For example: Type *No Fault Travel* and then press (Enter).

Be sure to check out our website: www.LutherMaddy.com to contact the author and see other resources available for this workbook.

Excel 2010: Beyond The Basics

Table of Contents

Lesson #1: Review 2
    Creating a workbook 2
    Formatting Cells 3
    Creating formulas 3
    Absolute Reference 4
Lesson #2: Working with Multiple Worksheets 8
    Inserting Worksheets 9
    Renaming sheets 9
    Copying information between worksheets 10
    Linking worksheets 14
    Using Functions when Linking worksheets 16
    Grouping Worksheets 17
    Ungrouping sheets 19
    Changing tab colors 19
    Skill Builder: Lesson #2 21
Lesson #3: Working with Functions 24
    The PMT() function 24
    The Vlookup() function 34
    Creating Named Ranges 35
    The IF() Function 40
    Nested If statements 41
    Conditional summing: SumIf() 42
    Skill Builder: Lesson #3 45
Lesson #4: Enhancing Excel Charts 48
    Adding and editing data series 51
    Combining Chart types 54
    Annotating charts 58
    Inserting images into charts 60
    Selecting chart elements 61
Lesson #5: Some very helpful features 66
    Using Auto Outline 66
    Inserting cell comments 68
    Protecting worksheets 70
    Using Data Validation and Input Messages 73
    Freezing worksheet panes 77
    Using the copy command to transpose data 79
Lesson #6: Excel Templates 82
    Using predefined templates 82
    Creating your own template 85
    Saving a workbook as a template 93

Lesson #1: Review

In this lesson you will review:

- *Cell formatting*
- *Basic Formulas*
- *Using Absolute Reference in formulas*

Lesson #1: Review

For this workbook it is assumed you already have some basic Excel knowledge and are now ready to add to your skills. You will begin this course by completing a simple workbook that will become the basis of many of the lessons in this workbook. In addition to using this for future lessons, creating this workbook will give you a quick review of some essential basic skills you should already have.

Creating a workbook

1. Start Excel and enter the information as shown in a new workbook.

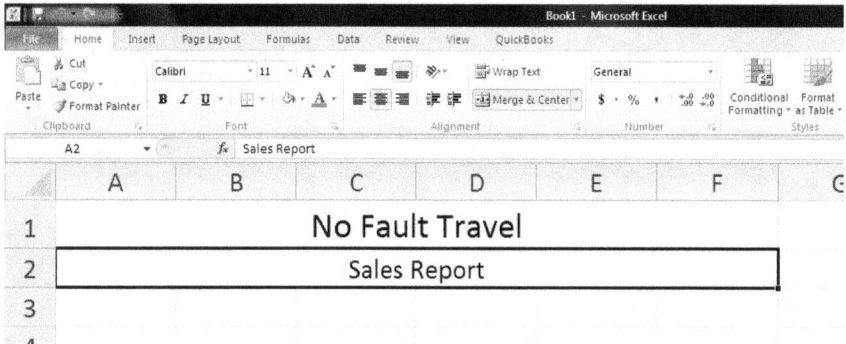

Remember you can use the Merge and Center tool on the Home tab to merge several cells into one, as shown in the example. The example worksheet has the zoom (View to Zoom) set at 200% for clarity. Your worksheet may appear differently depending on your own View settings.

2. Enter the remaining information as shown.

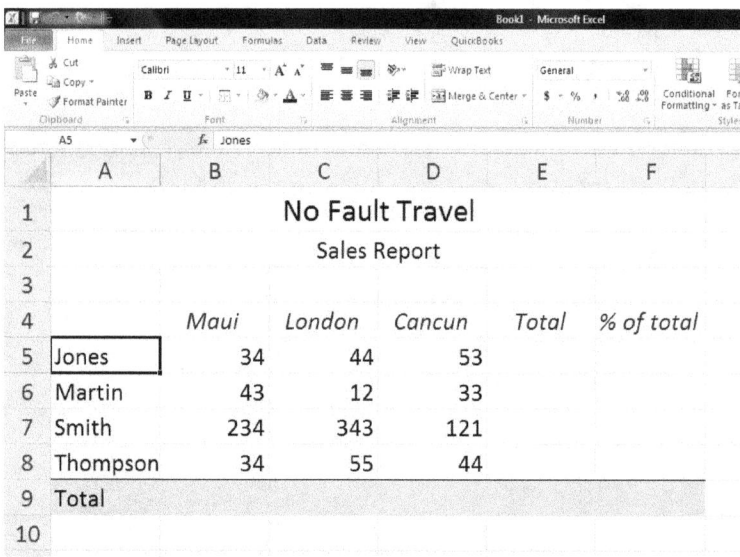

© 2014 Luther M. Maddy III

Formatting Cells

1. **Format the column headings in row four as shown, centered, dark blue font, and italicized, using the formatting tools on the Home tab.**

2. **Apply a top border and gray shading, fill color, to cells A9 through F9.**

    You can find the border and fill color tools on the Home tab.

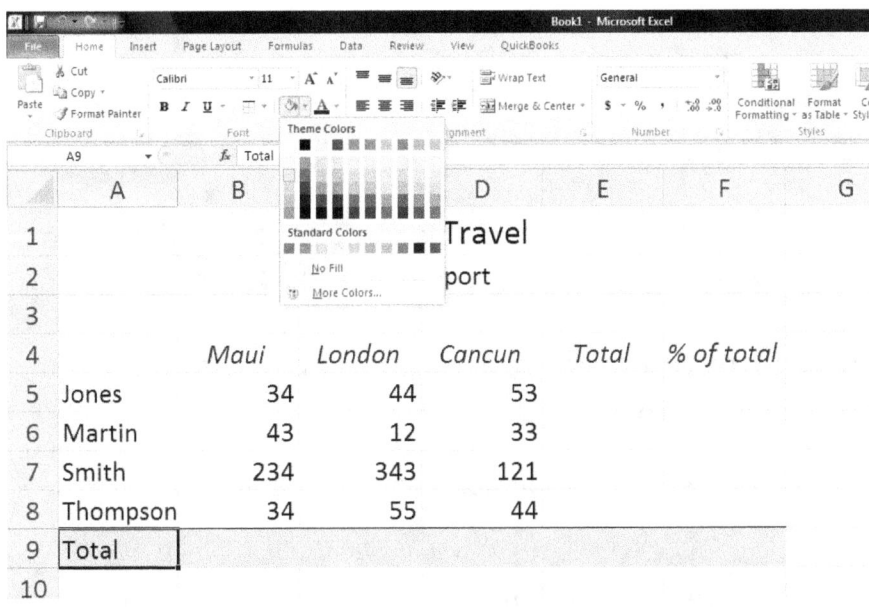

Creating formulas

You will now create formulas to compute the totals for each salesperson and each destination. You will use the Sum function to do this.

After creating the totals, you will create a formula that uses Absolute Reference to compute the percent of total for each sales person.

1. **Move to Cell B9 and double-click the AutoSum Σ AutoSum tool on the Home tab.**

    You should now see a total for the Maui destination. You will now copy this formula into London and Cancun destinations. Remember, when you copy a formula you are not copying the formula but what the formula does. In this case the formula adds the three cells above the total. This is the same thing you want it to do for the London and Cancun columns, so copying this formula will give you the correct result.

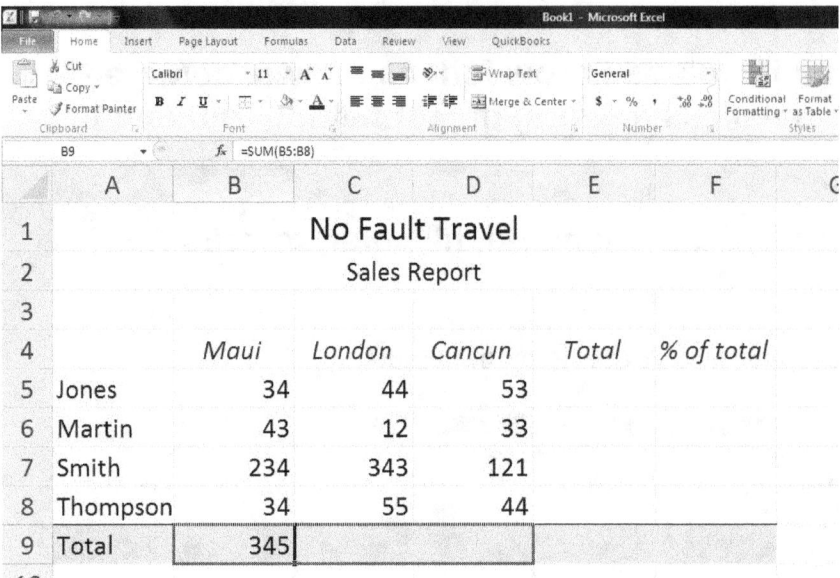

2. **Try using the fill handle, the skinny black plus at the right edge of the active cell, to copy the formula from B9 to C9 and D9.**

3. **Use the same procedure to create formulas for the totals for each salesperson in Column E.**

   You should now have totals for each salesperson and each destination.

Absolute Reference

Sometimes you want a cell to remain constant or absolute in a formula when it is copied. This will be the case with the percent of total formulas. To compute the % for each salesperson, their total will be divided by the grand total (E9). For example, the formula for cell E5, "the Jones row", will be E5/E9. Likewise, each remaining salesperson will have their total divided by E9 to compute their percentage. Rather than having to create a formula for each salesperson, using the Absolute Reference feature will allow you to create the formula for Jones and then copy it to Martin, Smith, and Thompson without having to change it.

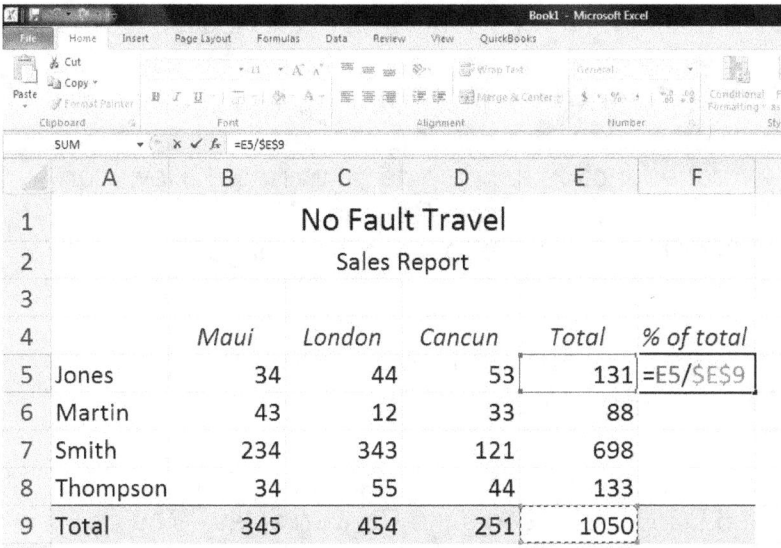

1. **In cell F5, enter the formula =E5/$E$9.**

   When creating formulas manually, you always precede them with =. And, as you should recall, the dollar signs ($) inform Excel not to change this cell when you copy the formula. You may also recall that you could use the shortcut key (F4) to add the dollar signs after typing cell E9.

2. **Use the fill handle and copy the formula in cell F5 to cells F6 through F9.**

   Your worksheet should now appear as that below. Copying formulas using the fill handle will also copy cell formatting. This results in the shading (fill) being removed from cell F9. You can easily add it again if you like.

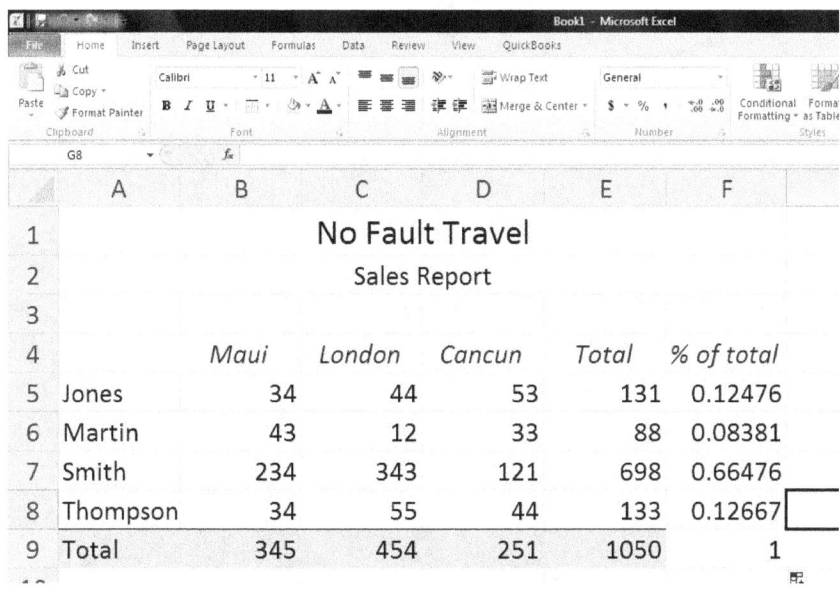

You will add additional cell formatting, currency and % in a later lesson.

3. **In cell A12 enter the label *Average sales for tropical locations.***

You will now use Excel's Average function to compute an average. However, this average will be for only the destinations of Maui and Cancun. These cells are noncontiguous (not together), so rather than dragging to select one range, you will average two cell ranges in one formula.

4. **In A13, type the formula to compute the average sales for Tropical locations, *=average(B5:B8,D5:D8).***

The first set of cell references, B5:B8, represent the Maui sales. The comma (,) represents a break in the range, and D5:D8 represents the Cancun sales. You can use multiple ranges in other Excel functions such as Sum, Max, or Min.

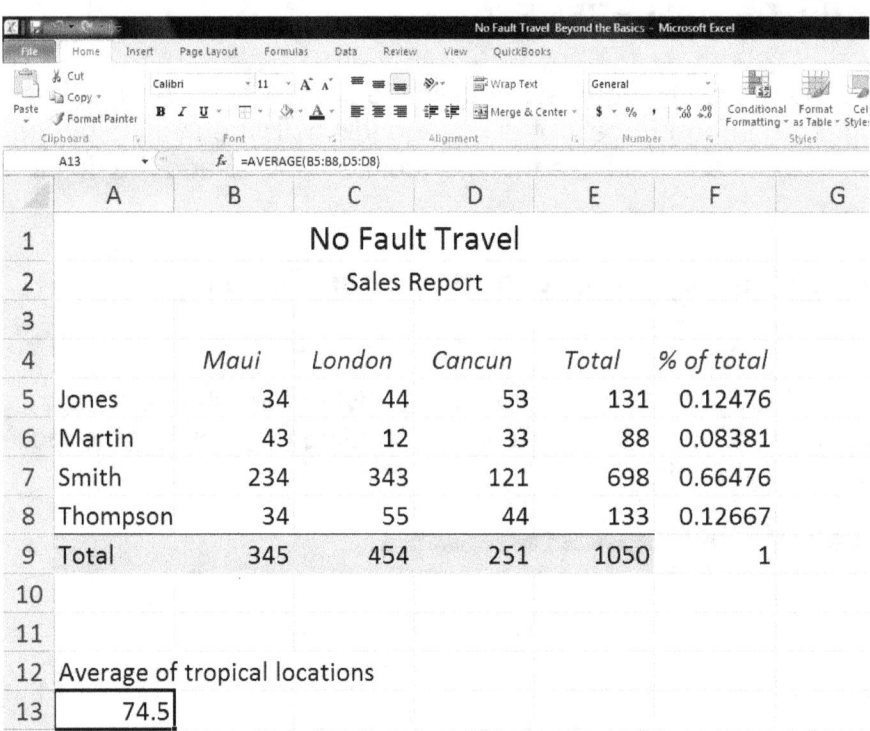

5. **Save the completed file as *No Fault Travel.***

You have now successfully completed your review. You will continue to build on this file as you continue this course.

Lesson #2: Working with Multiple Worksheets

In this lesson you will learn to:

Insert worksheets
Rename worksheets
Group worksheets
Link worksheets

Excel 2010: Beyond The Basics

Lesson #2: Working with Multiple Worksheets

When you create a new workbook in Excel, you have three worksheets available. Each sheet is named, Sheet1 through Sheet3, and the sheet tabs at the bottom of the workbook allow you to switch to another worksheet.

A worksheet is essentially another page within a workbook. You can use additional worksheets any way you like. Multiple worksheets are especially useful for computing the same values for several time periods, such as months, days, or years. You could also use worksheets to separate different departments, vendors, or customers.

Excel allows you to insert additional worksheets or delete unneeded sheets. In this lesson, you will use multiple worksheets to track No Fault Travel trip sales values for three different months.

1. **Open the *No Fault Travel* workbook you created in the review lesson.**

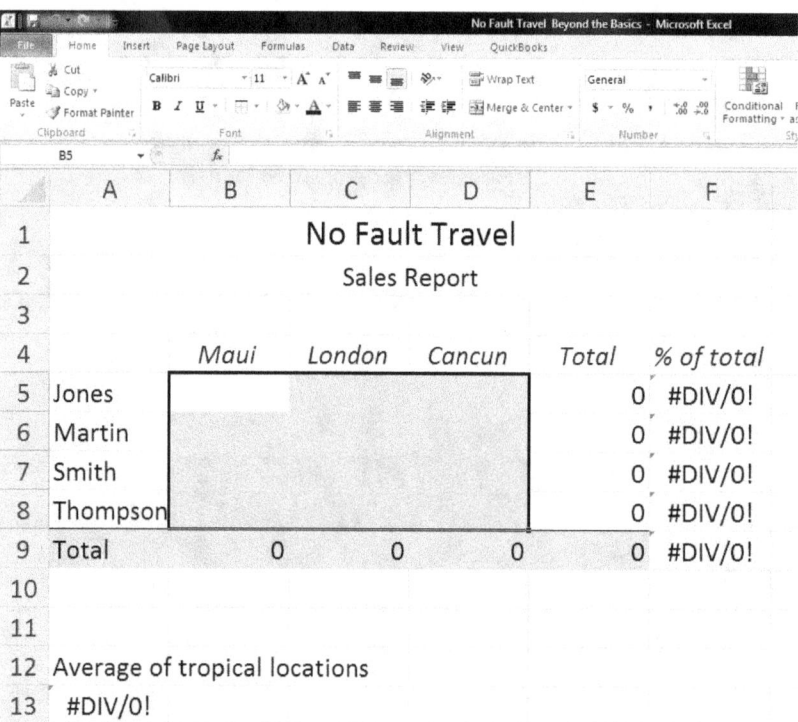

2. **Select cells B5 through D8 and press the (Delete) key to erase the current values.**

You will use this worksheet as a template to create the worksheets for the additional months. Be careful that your selection does not go beyond this range. You only want to erase the data, not any of the formulas. Leaving the formulas intact will save you time and effort.

3. Use the Save As command and save this workbook as *Travel Report*.

Using the Save As command ensures that the original No Fault Travel workbook remains as it was.

Inserting Worksheets

Each new Excel workbook has only 3 worksheets. However, you can add additional sheets, if you need them. When you insert a new worksheet, Excel will place the new sheet after the last existing worksheet.

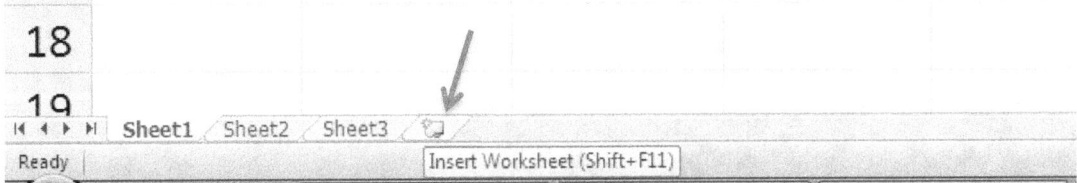

1. Click the Insert Worksheet control.

You should now see that Excel created a new worksheet after Sheet3. It named this worksheet Sheet4 because it is the fourth sheet added to the Workbook. After Excel created this new worksheet, it made that worksheet active. You can move from sheet to sheet by clicking on its sheet tab.

Renaming sheets

If you are using several worksheets in a workbook, referring to them by their default name (Sheet1, etc..) may cause confusion and you may even forget what sheet stores what information. Fortunately, you can easily rename the worksheets in a workbook. Renaming worksheets helps the user understand what each worksheet refers to. It also makes creating formulas based on values from other worksheets easier too.

One of the easiest ways to rename a worksheet is to simply double-click on its tab. This will select the existing name and you can then type the new name. You can also rename a worksheet by accessing the sheet's shortcut menu by right-clicking on its tab.

1. Double-click on the tab for Sheet1. When Sheet1 is selected, type *Jan* and press (Enter).

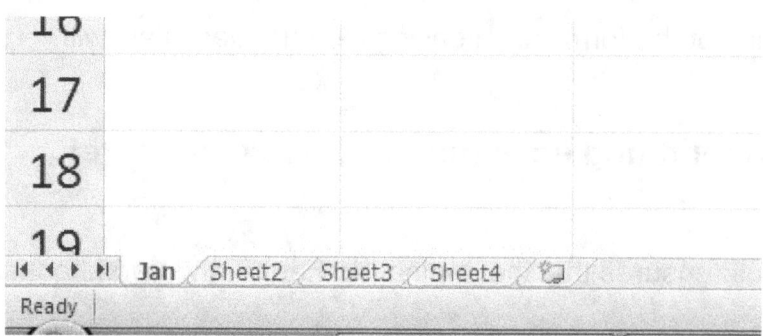

2. **Use the same method to rename the remaining sheets *Feb, Mar* and *Quarter Total* as shown below.**

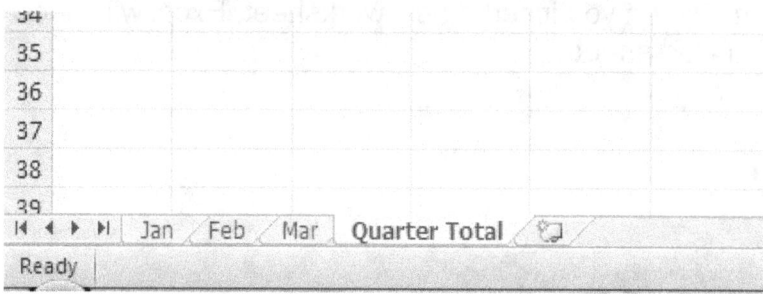

Copying information between worksheets

The January worksheet has the template with the formulas already created. All you need to do on this worksheet it enter the month's data and the totals, percentages, and average will be computed using the formulas you already created.

You will also be able to use this same template for the February and March worksheets. So, rather than entering all the information manually for each of these additional worksheets, you will just copy the template from the January worksheet to the February and March worksheets. When you do copy from one sheet to another, the formulas will adjust to the new worksheet.

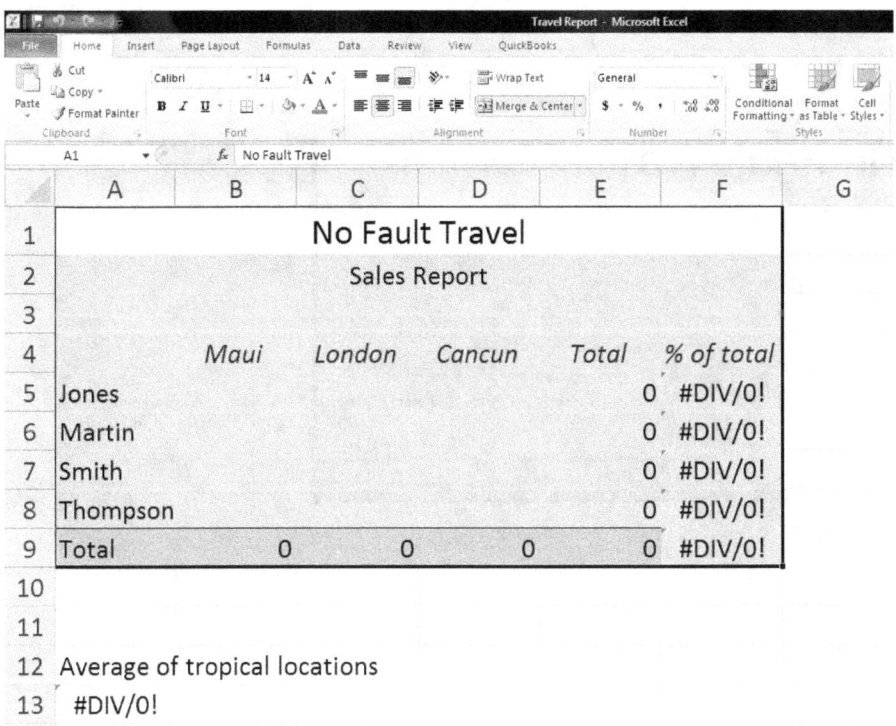

1. **Click the January worksheet tab to make it active. Then, select cells A1:F9 and then choose the Copy command.**

You have now placed the data and the formulas from the cells you copied into the clipboard. You will paste this information into the other worksheets that need this template. This selection does not include the average information. You will not copy that information at this time, although you certainly could and it would work properly on the new sheet.

	A	B	C	D	E	F	G
	A1		fx	No Fault Travel			
1	No Fault Travel						
2	Sales Report						
3							
4		Maui	London	Cancun	Total	% of total	
5	Jones				0	#DIV/0!	
6	Martin				0	#DIV/0!	
7	Smith				0	#DIV/0!	
8	Thompson				0	#DIV/0!	
9	Total	0	0	0	0	#DIV/0!	

2. Switch to the Feb sheet, make sure A1 is the active cell and then paste.

You pasted beginning at cell A1 so that the cell addresses will be consistent from one sheet to another.

3. Move to cell A1 in the Mar sheet and paste again.

You should have a copy of the template in the Jan, Feb and Mar worksheets. You did not paste this information into the Quarter Total sheet because it will contain different information than the other three worksheets.

The cells you copied in the January worksheet will still be selected. You will also see the dashed marquee around the cells you copied. You can remove this marquee by pressing the (Esc) key or just by entering new data.

4. **Move to the Jan sheet and enter the values shown below.**

	A	B	C	D
1		No Fault Trave		
2		Sales Report		
3				
4		Maui	London	Cancun
5	Jones	2	11	4
6	Martin	5	0	3
7	Smith	2	4	1
8	Thompson	4	2	3

The total and % of total cells will be computed for you as you are entering these values because you left the formulas when you erased the data.

5. **Enter the values below into the Feb worksheet.**

	Maui	London	Cancun
Jones	6	10	4
Martin	9	2	1
Smith	12	11	0
Thompson	3	8	9

6. **Enter the values below into the Mar worksheet.**

	Maui	London	Cancun
Jones	8	5	7
Martin	12	10	6
Smith	5	7	9
Thompson	0	1	2

You now have values in the worksheets for all three months. You will now create formulas in the Quarter Total worksheet that add the values from all three months.

7. **Copy cells A5:A9 from the Jan worksheet and paste the copy beginning at cell A5 in the Quarter Total sheet.**

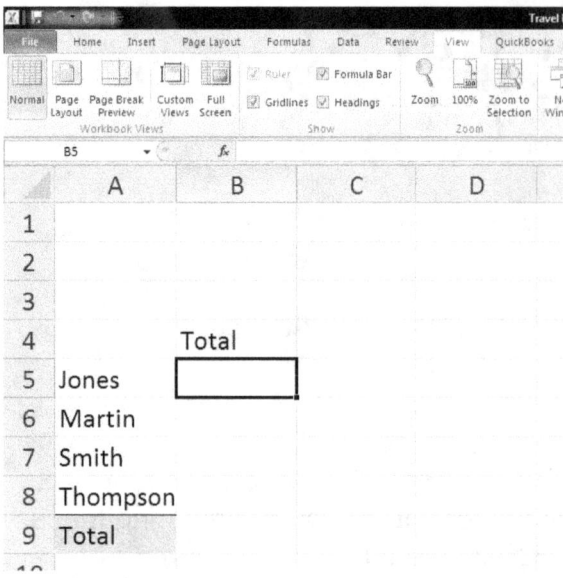

8. **In cell B4 of the Quarter Total worksheet type *Total* and then move to cell B5.**

Linking worksheets

The Quarter Total worksheet will display the total of all three months for each salesperson. You will do this by creating a formula. This formula will be linked to the other worksheets. Because these formulas will be linked to the values in other worksheets, the results of these formulas will change if the values in the other worksheets should change.

To create a formula that refers to a cell on another worksheet you can either type the formula or you can use the "point and click" method. Regardless of the method you use the syntax is the same. The syntax for a formula that refers to a cell on a different worksheet is: =Sheetname!cellAddress. In other words to create a formula that refers to cell E5 on the Jan worksheet, the formula would be: =Jan!E5.

When you create linking formulas manually, you have to remember to separate the sheet name and the cell address with an exclamation point (!). You also need to ensure that you spell each sheet name exactly in the formula. Using the "point and click" method to enter formulas eliminates some of the potential for error because Excel does the typing instead of you. This workbook will step you through using the "point and click" method to create a formula that adds the totals of all three months on the Quarter Total worksheet.

1. **Move to the Quarter Total worksheet and in cell B5, begin a formula by pressing the (=) key.**

    This formula will sum all the sales for Jones. Instead of typing the cell addresses, you will use the "point and click" method.

2. **Click on the Jan worksheet tab and then click on cell E5.**

    You should notice that the formula bar displays the sheet name and the cell address.

3. **Type a (+) and then click on the Feb worksheet tab.**

    The name of this tab should also be added to the formula you are creating.

4. **Click on cell E5 in the Feb tab and then type another (+).**
    You will now complete the formula by adding the March total for Jones.

5. **Click on the Mar tab, click on cell E5 and then press (Enter).**

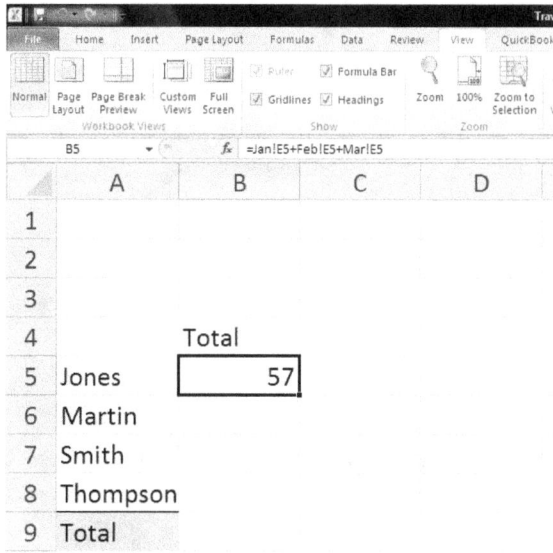

The result of the formula appears in cell B5. If you move back into cell B5 you should now see the completed formula in the formula bar. If your formula does not appear as it should, move back into cell B5 and repeat the process. Some of the most common errors users make when creating these formulas is forgetting to click on the cell after selecting the worksheet and adding a plus (+) after clicking on the last cell rather than pressing the (Enter) key.

Using Functions when Linking worksheets

In addition to creating the formula as you did, you could have also used the Sum function to build the formula. Doing so you would create the formula as: =Sum(Jan:Mar!E5). This would be a more practical approach for adding the values in several worksheets. Typing this formula works fine as long as you have the sheet names typed properly. You could also use other functions when linking worksheets such as Average, Count, Min, and Max.

1.   Use the fill handle to copy the formula from B5 to B6:B9.

This is a copyable formula. The cell addresses are relative and adjust as they should when you copy the formula. Sheet names are absolute and do not change when you copy the formula, which is exactly what you want when copying this formula on the same worksheet.

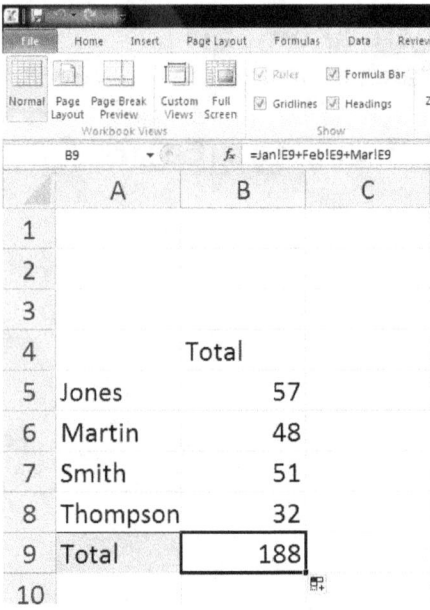

2.   Move to the Jan worksheet and change the Maui value for Jones from 2 to 22.

3. **Move to the Quarter Total worksheet and verify that it now reflects the changed value.**

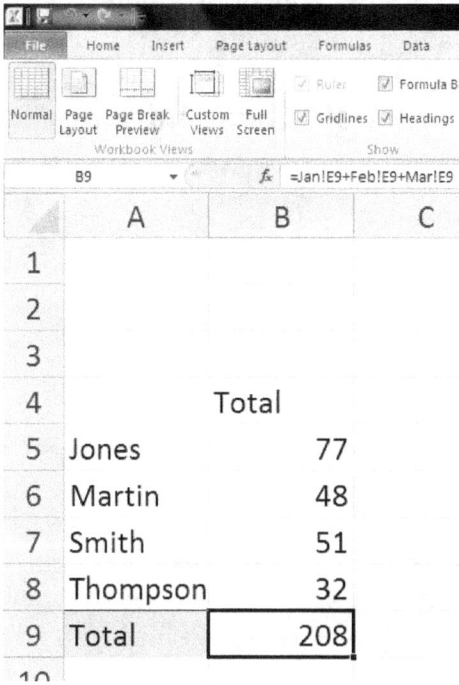

4. **Save the Travel Report worksheet.**

This workbook is not yet complete but saving at this point reminds you to practice the habit of saving your work periodically. Save early and often and avoid recreating your worksheets.

Grouping Worksheets

There may be times when you want to do the same thing in all worksheets. For example, maybe you would like to italicize some cells or change the color of other cells in every worksheet. If you had formatted the January worksheet exactly as you wanted all the others to appear before you copied the data, those worksheets would have the same formatting. Now, however, if you change formatting on one worksheet, you will have to repeat the process on every other worksheet individually, unless you use the grouping feature.

Without the grouping feature you would have to enhance those cells in each worksheet, one at a time. By grouping the worksheets, you can change the formatting of one worksheet and have all the other sheets get the same formatting changes. Changing formatting options works well with the grouping feature, but only when the grouped worksheets have the same information in the same cells, as the Travel Report workbook does.

Grouping worksheets is very easy. You can group worksheets by clicking on the first worksheet tab and then, while holding down the (Shift) key, click on the last worksheet to be included in the group. If the worksheets are not contiguous, you can use the Control+Click method to select multiple non-adjacent worksheets.

1. **Click on the Jan worksheet tab. Press and hold the (Shift) key and then click the Mar tab.**

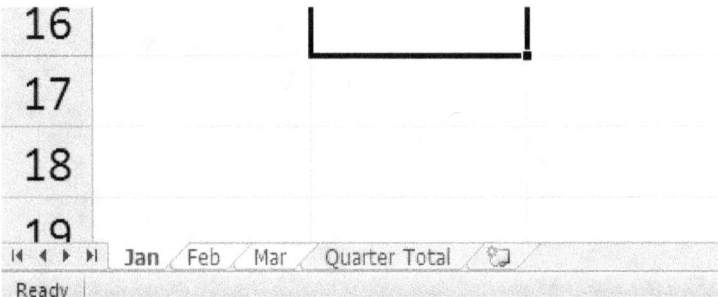

You notice that all three sheet tabs now appear selected. While the worksheets are grouped, whatever you do to one worksheet will be done to all. That includes changing values and formulas, so be very careful what changes you make when you have multiple worksheets selected.

2. **Select cells B4:F4, the titles in Row 4.**

Even though you cannot see it, Excel has selected these cells in all three worksheets.

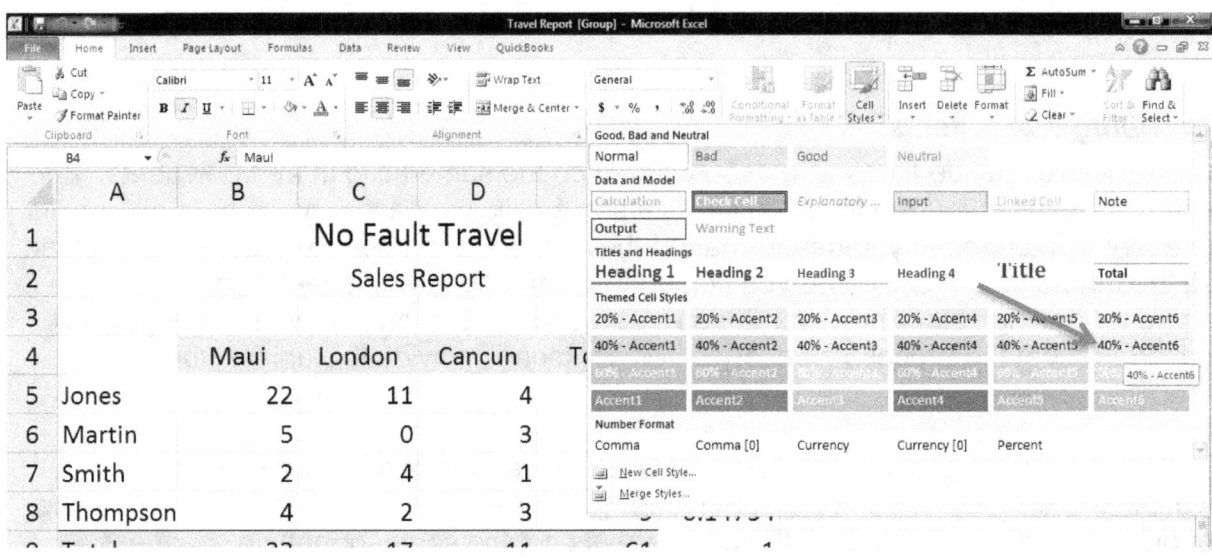

3. **Click the Cell Styles tool on the Home tab and then select 40% Accent6.**

If you click on the sheet tabs for Feb and Mar you will see that the titles in each worksheet now have the same cell style.

Ungrouping sheets

When you no longer need the worksheets to be grouped, you should be careful to un-group them. If not, you could accidentally change data in several worksheets. To ungroup worksheets you can simply click on a sheet that is not part of the group. In the event that all sheets are grouped, you can right-click any sheet tab and choose Ungroup Sheets from the shortcut menu.

1. **Right-click the Feb worksheet tab.**

You should now see the Worksheet shortcut menu.

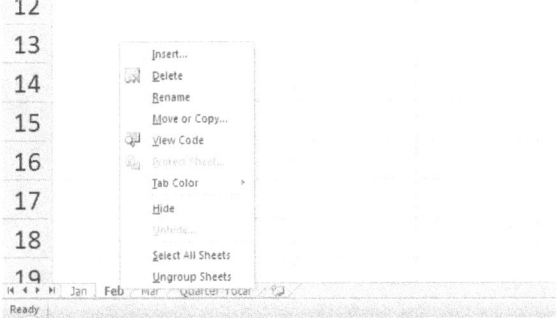

2. **Choose Ungroup Sheets from the shortcut menu.**

You should notice that none of the sheets are grouped.

Changing tab colors

In addition to renaming worksheets, you can also change their colors. This makes them easier to identify when you are working with several worksheets. To change the color of a sheet tab, you can right-click any sheet tab and choose Tab Color from the shortcut menu.

1. **Right-click the Jan worksheet and choose Tab Color.**

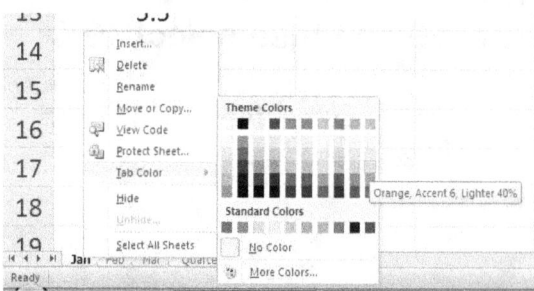

You should now see the available colors for sheet tabs. You can also choose the More Colors… option to choose from an even larger list of tab colors.

2.   Choose Orange, Accent 6, Light 40% for the January tab.

The color you choose is not all that important for this lesson. You can choose different colors if you like. After choosing a tab color, you will not see the color change until you select another worksheet tab.

3.   Change the tab colors for the remaining worksheets to any colors you desire.

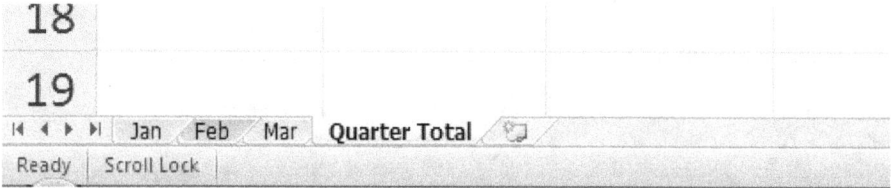

4.   Save the workbook after making these changes and then Close it.

Saving the workbook with the Save or Save as commands saves all the worksheets, not just the one that is currently selected.

Skill Builder: Lesson #2

In this skill builder you will create a monthly budget workbook. You will create worksheets for January, February, and March. You will then create a summary worksheet that will average your spending for those three months.

1. **Create a new workbook; entering the following worksheet on Sheet1.**

   Be sure to use a formula for the Total cell.

   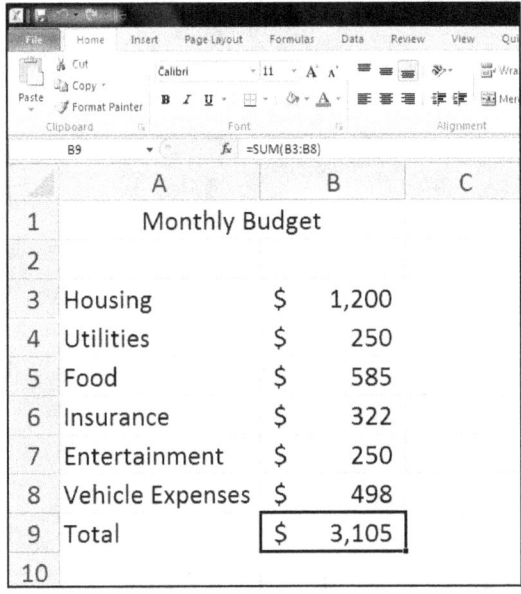

2. **Insert another worksheet. Then, copy this information to Sheet2, Sheet3, and Sheet4.**

3. **Rename the sheets *January*, *February*, *March* and *First Quarter Average*.**

   Rename the sheets in the order listed, so the first sheet is January and the last is First Quarter Average.

4. **Erase the values and total on the First Quarter Average sheet. Then, create a formula in cell B3 that averages all three month's housing values.**

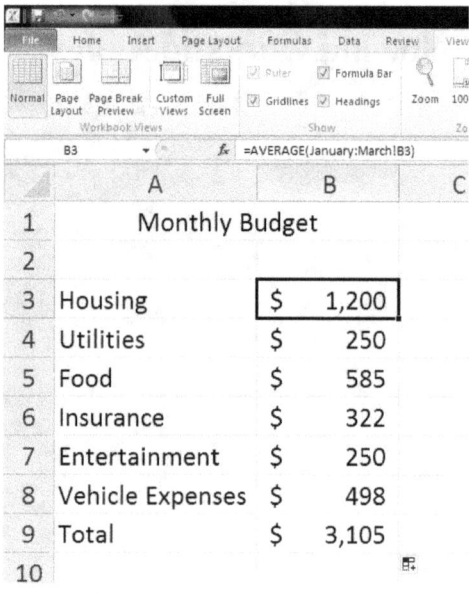

5. **Copy the formula from B3 to B4 through B9.**

   Your worksheet should appear as the above. Since all three months have the same values for each category, the average is the same as all the other values.

6. **Change some of the budget item values on both the February and March worksheets.**

Now, as you return to the First Quarter Average worksheet, the averages will be different than the monthly values.

7. **Save this workbook as *Monthly Budget* and close it.**

Lesson #3: Working with Functions

In this lesson you will learn to use the following functions:
- *PMT*
- *IF*
- *SumIF*
- *Vlookup*

Lesson #3: Working with Functions

The functions available in Excel make it easy to perform mathematical operations that would be, at best, very difficult without them. Up to this point you are familiar with at least the Sum and Average functions. Excel has many more very useful functions for just about every computation you may ever want.

Excel's functions are grouped by category, such and Financial, Statistical, or Math and Trig. Within each category are several useful functions. In this lesson you will get just a small glimpse of some of the power within Excel's functions.

The PMT() function

The PMT() function allows you to compute loan payments based on a fixed payment amount and fixed interest rate. If you know the amount of the loan, the interest rate and the loan length, Excel's PMT() function will do the rest. After you have computed a loan payment, it is also then very easy to create a complete loan amortization schedule.

You will now use Excel's PMT() function to compute a loan payment then create a loan amortization schedule. An amortization schedule displays the breakdown for each payment of the loan, including the amount applied to interest and principal. It also displays the loan balance after each scheduled payment.

1. **In a new workbook, enter the labels as shown below. Change the column width of Column A as needed.**

   To change column width you can double-click the column's edge to have Excel adjust the column to the widest value or label in the column. Or, you can click and drag to manually adjust the width.

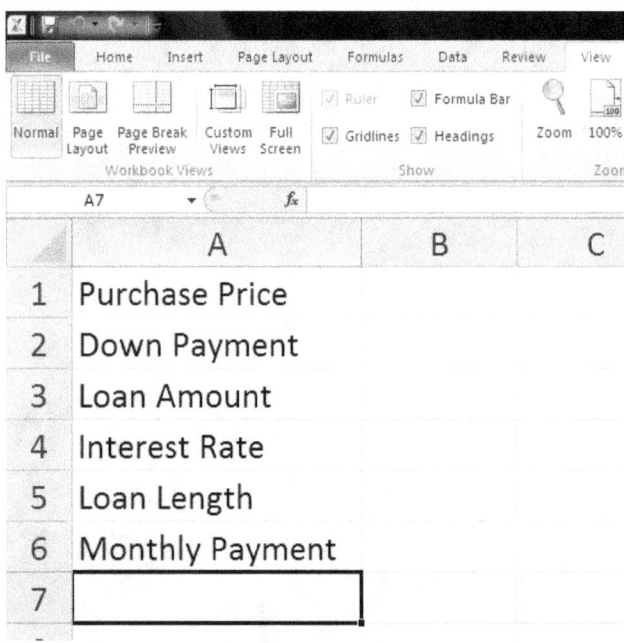

2. **Create a formula in cell B3 that subtracts the Down Payment from the Purchase Price.**

The computed value in cell B3 will be the amount that the PMT() function uses to calculate a loan payment. The formula is =B1-B2.

3. **Enter the values as shown below. Format the values as shown.**

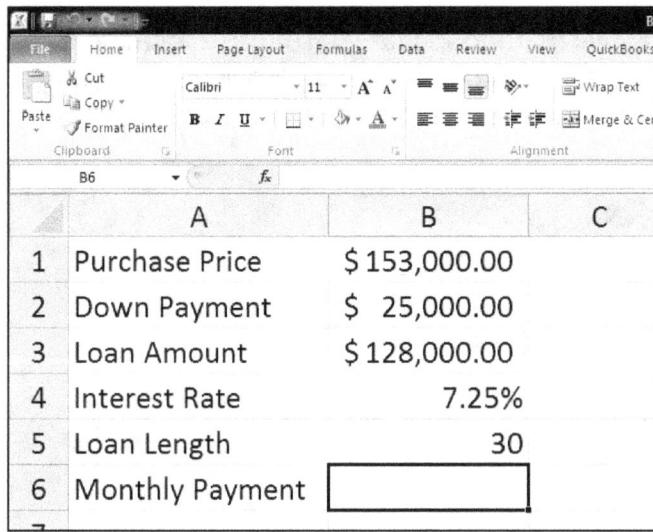

It is not necessary to enter values before creating the formula that computes the loan payment. Placing values in the cells first will make the formula easier to understand as you create it. The loan length is in years, making this a 30 year loan.

4. **Move to cell B6 and then click the Insert Function tool on the Formula bar.**

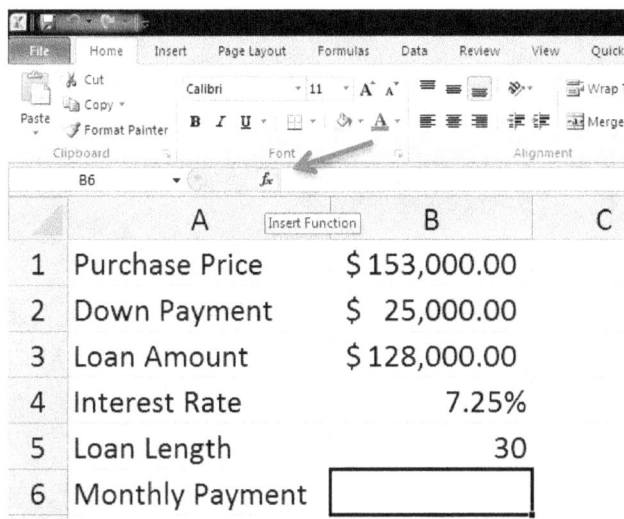

If you apply currency formatting before entering the loan length, Excel may automatically add currency formatting to this cell. You can remove the formatting by clicking the Clear tool on the Home tab and then choosing Clear Formats.

As soon as you click the Insert Function tool, Excel will display the Insert Function dialog box. By default Excel shows the "Most Recently Used" category. As you use functions, Excel will add those functions to this category. This makes it very easy to find the functions you commonly use.

The first time you use a function you will need to locate it. To make locating a particular function easier, Excel breaks them down into categories. However, if you are unsure which category the function you are looking for may be in, Excel has an All category that lists functions alphabetically.

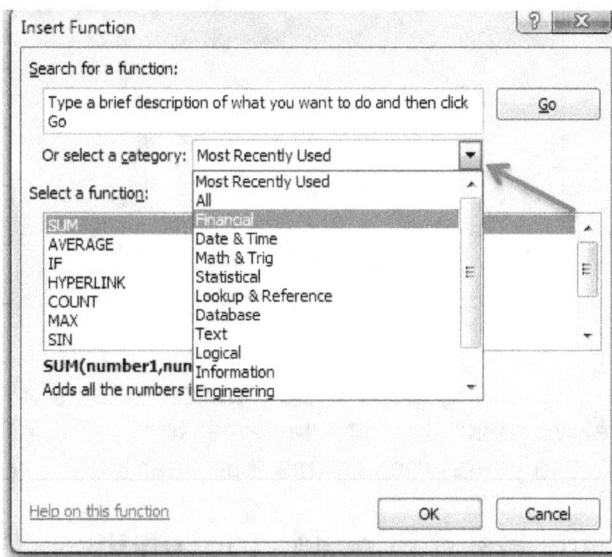

5. Click the Select a category drop down list and choose the Financial category.

The PMT() function is located in the Financial category.

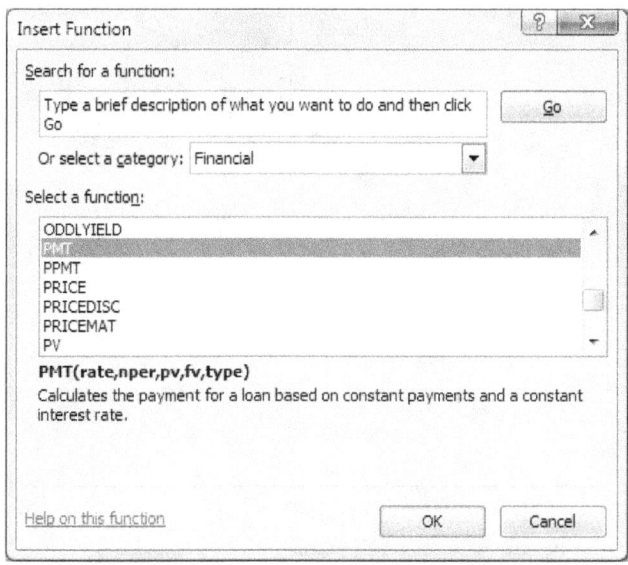

6. **In the Function Name column, select the PMT function and click OK.**

   Excel will now display the function arguments dialog box. This dialog box allows you to specify the arguments or parameters you want to use for this function. If the data in the worksheet is hidden by the dialog box, you can easily move the dialog box out of the way by clicking and dragging on its title bar.

7. **If needed, click and drag the title bar of the "function assistant" dialog box and drag it right so you can see the values in the worksheet.**

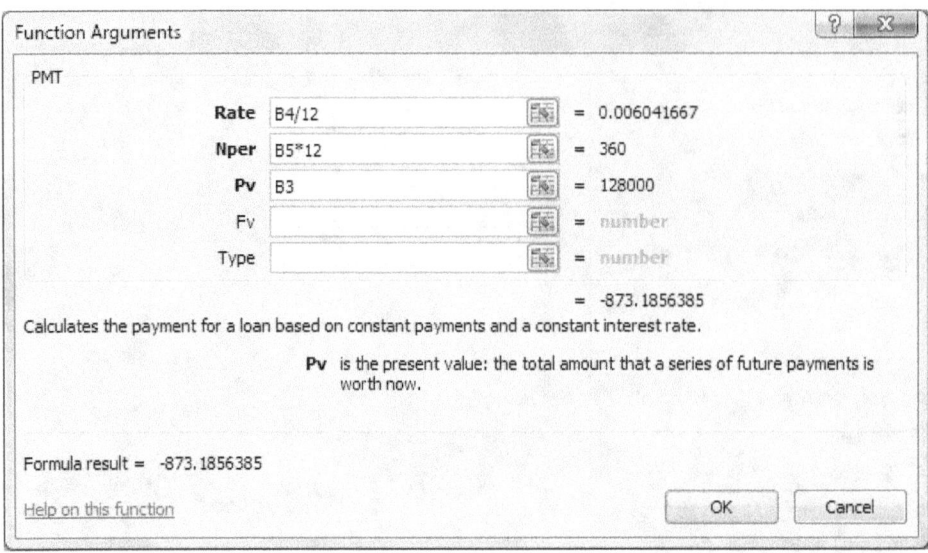

8. **Enter the formula as shown in the Function Arguments dialog box.**

    Use the (Tab) key, not the (Enter) key, to move from field to field.

    Notice that this formula divides the interest rate by 12 and multiplies the loan length by 12. This is to change both of these into monthly rather than annual values. When dealing with formulas that reference time, all time elements should be the same. By changing these values to monthly values, they will match the resulting payment, which is a monthly payment rather than annual payment.

9. **Click OK to complete the monthly payment formula.**

    Excel will now display the loan payment amount in cell B6. You may notice that Excel displays this amount in red. This is because Excel has computed this as a negative number because it is an outflow (a payment). You will use this value to create the amortization schedule. Doing so will be easier if it is a positive rather than negative number. To convert a negative number to a positive number you simply multiply the value by -1.

Excel 2010: Beyond The Basics

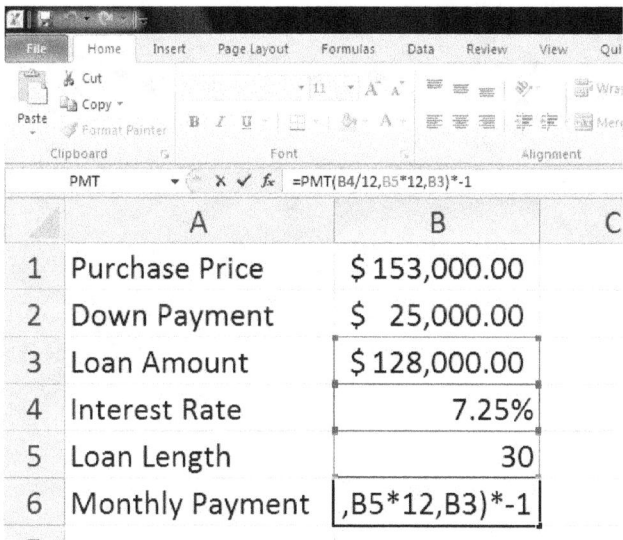

10. In cell B6, click in the formula bar and add *-1* at the very end of the formula and press (Enter).

Multiplying a negative value by -1 changes the payment into a positive value.

You will now create a loan amortization schedule using the values you just entered. After you have created it, you may use it for your own values if you like.

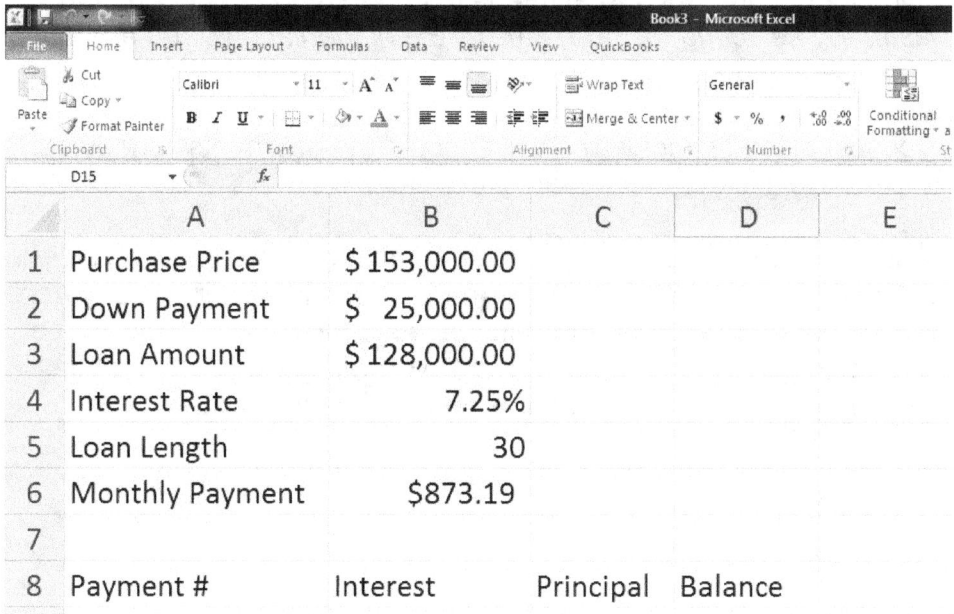

11. In cell A8 enter *Payment #*. In cell B8 enter *Interest*. In cell C8 enter *Principal* and then enter *Balance* in cell D8 as shown.

	A	B	C	D	E
5	Loan Length	30			
6	Monthly Payment	$873.19			
7					
8	Payment #	Interest		Principal	Balance
9	1				
10	2				
11	3				
12	4				
13	5				
14	6				
15	7				
16	8				
17	9				
18	10				
19	11				

12. Use the fill handle to create incrementing numbers that begin with 1 in cell A9 and end with 360 in cell A368.

Hint: To use the fill handle to increment the numbers you will need to type the 1 and the 2. Then, select both cells and then use the fill handle to drag down to cell A368. To increment numbers, Excel needs to understand the pattern you want it to replicate. By selecting the 1 and the 2, Excel then knows you are trying to increment the values by one.

The numbers you just placed in column A will become the payments scheduled for this loan, 360 in all because it is a 30 year loan.

You are now ready to create the formulas for the amortization schedule. You will begin by creating the formals for payment #1. The formulas you create for this payment cannot be successfully copied for the other payments because the relationships will be different. So, after creating the formulas for payment #1, you will then create formulas for payment #2. This payment will have relationships you can copy to all the other scheduled payments.

Excel 2010: Beyond The Basics

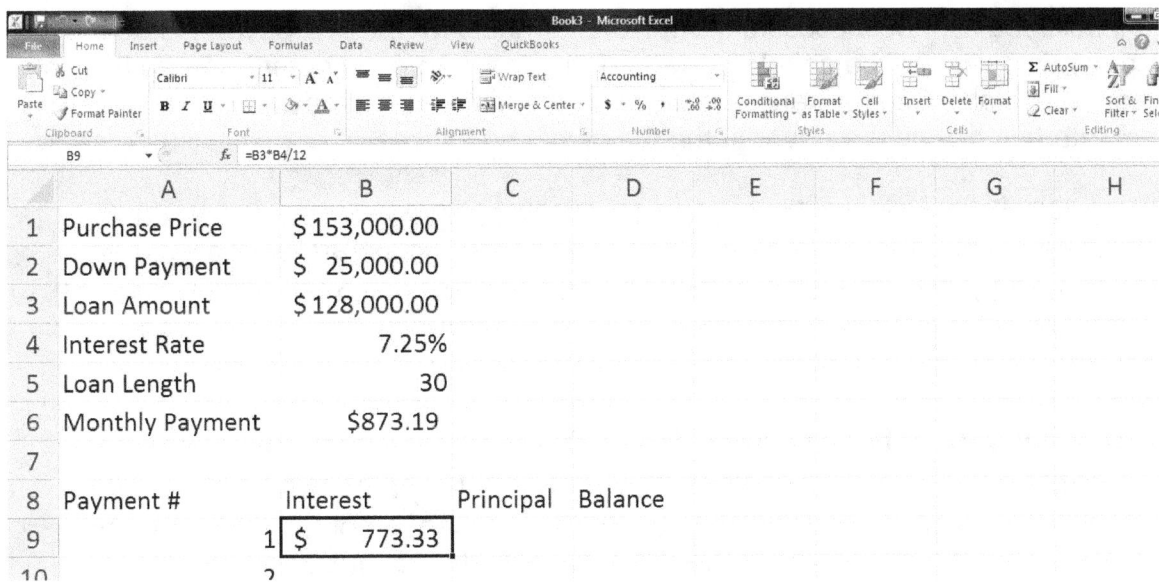

13. **In cell B9, create a formula that computes one month's interest for the original loan amount:** *=B3*B4/12*

    Once again you are dividing the result by 12 to compute only one month's value.

14. **In cell C9, create a formula that computes how much of payment #1 is applied to principal.**
    This formula is *=B6-B9.*

15. **In cell D9, create a formula that computes the loan balance after making the first payment**
    This formula is *=B3-C9.*

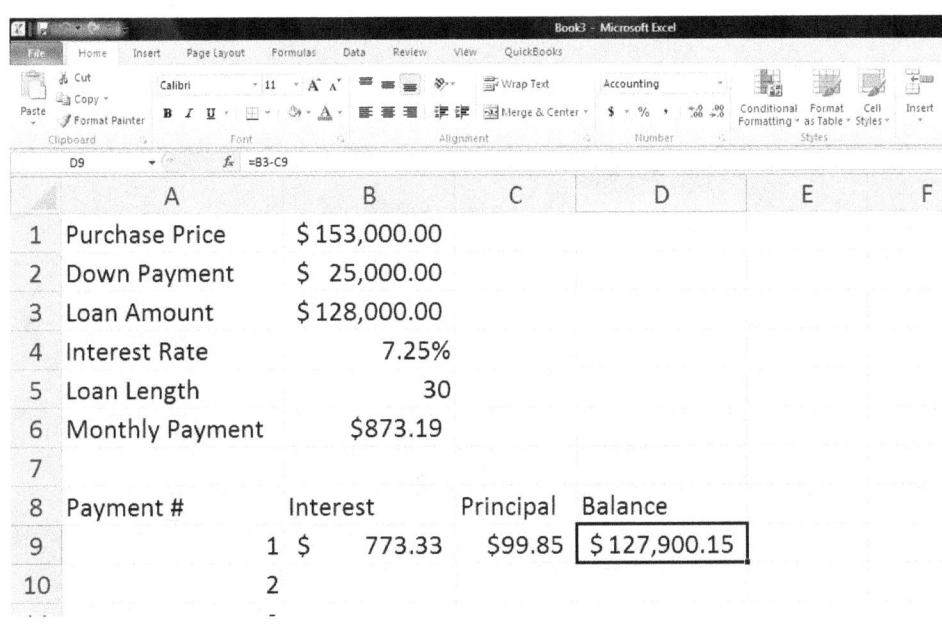

While you cannot successfully copy the formulas for the first payment into the other payments, you will be able to copy the formulas from payment #2. To do this you will need to use absolute reference because all these additional payments will use the interest rate and payment amount at the top of the worksheet.

16.   In cell B10 enter a formula of =D9*$B$4/12.
This formula refers to the balance after making the first payment. The loan amount is no longer the loan balance after making the first payment. This formula also uses absolute reference since all additional payment formulas will use cell B4 as the interest rate.

17.   In cell C10 enter =$B$6-B10 as the formula that computes how much of payment number 2 is applied to principal.
This formula subtracts the interest from the payment amount. The payment amount is a constant and will not change as you copy this formula.

18.   In cell D10 enter =D9-C10 as the formula to compute the balance after making payment #2.
The loan balance formula now has a relationship you can copy to the other payments. This formula subtracts the principal amount of this payment from the previous balance.

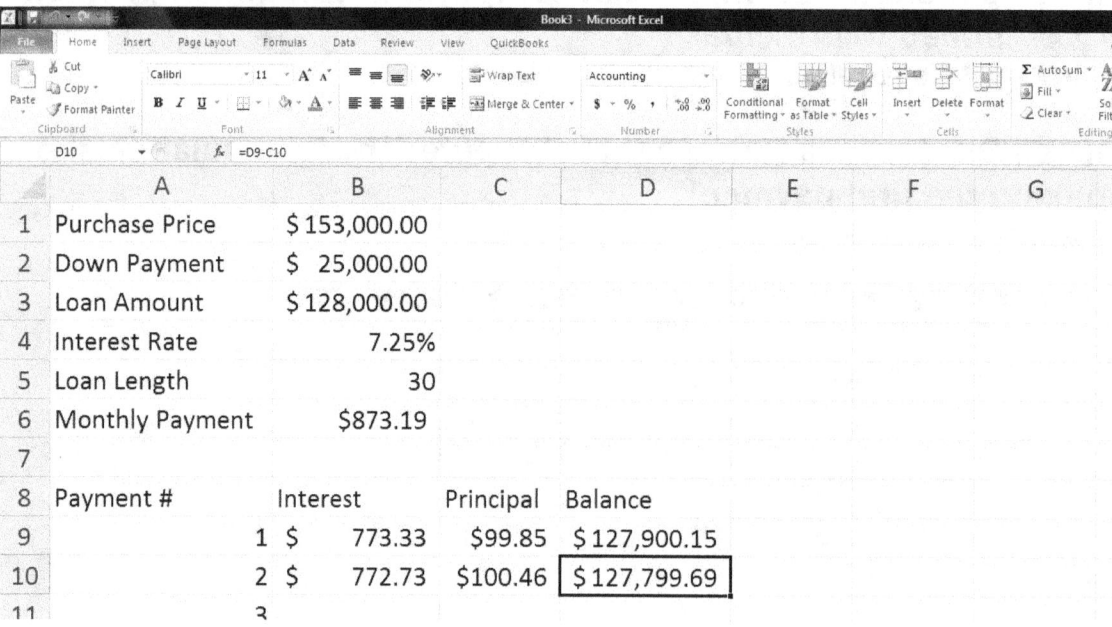

You are now ready to copy the formulas from payment #2 for the additional payments. To do this you will use the fill handle, but you will also be introduced to a shortcut you can use when copying formulas with the fill handle.

8	Payment #	Interest	Principal	Balance
9	1	$ 773.33	$99.85	$127,900.15
10	2	$ 772.73	$100.46	$127,799.69

19. Select cells B10:D10.

You are selecting the formulas you just created for payment #2. Remember, to select cells, use the "fat white plus" rather than the fill handle.

20. Keeping these cells selected, double-click the fill handle in cell D10.

You should now see that Excel copied the formulas all the way down to payment #360. When you double-click the fill handle, Excel will then copy the formula until it sees a blank row. Since you already have numbers down to 360, Excel copied the formula up to payment #360.

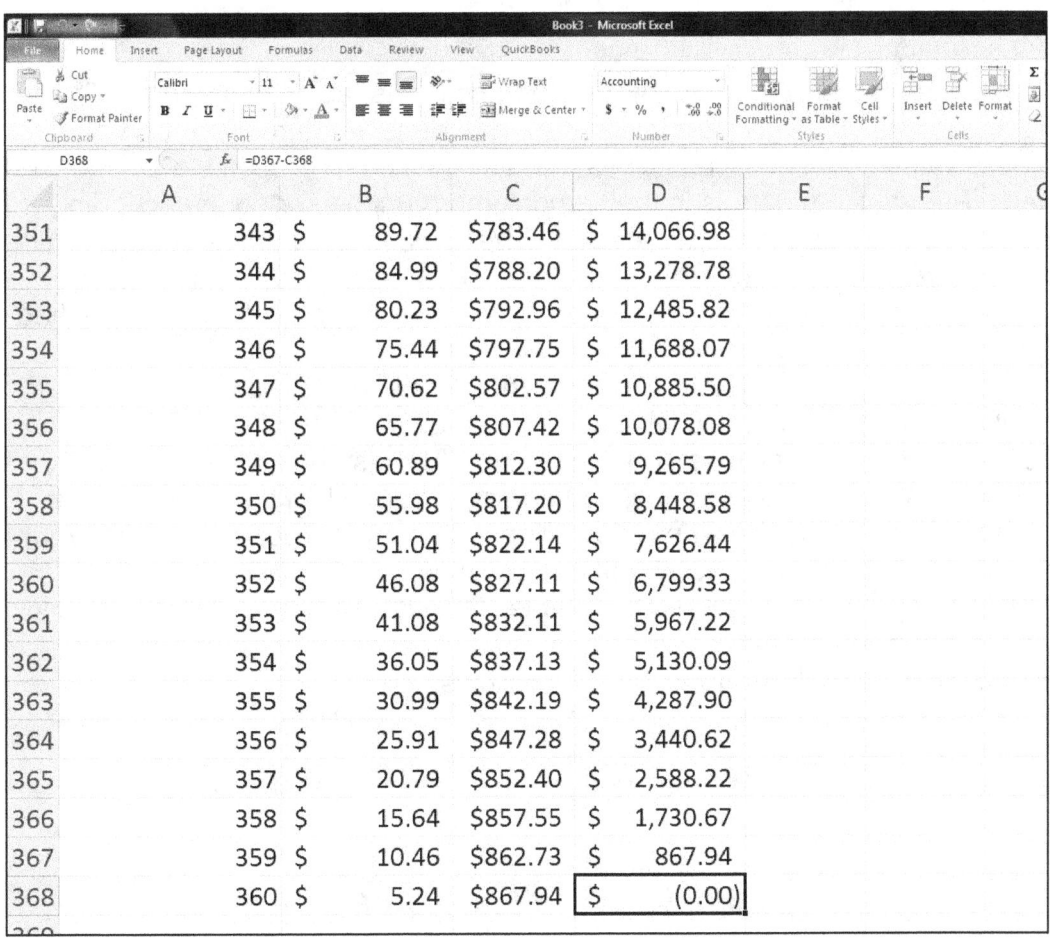

21. Save this workbook as *Loan Amortization* and then close it.

The Vlookup() function

The Vlookup function allows you to create formulas that look up values located in a table. For example you may use the Vlookup function to look up prices for a particular item based on its part number. Or, you may want to look up an employee's hourly wage based on their employee number. Once you have looked up a value you can then use the resulting values in formulas. This function is very useful for creating invoices or estimates.

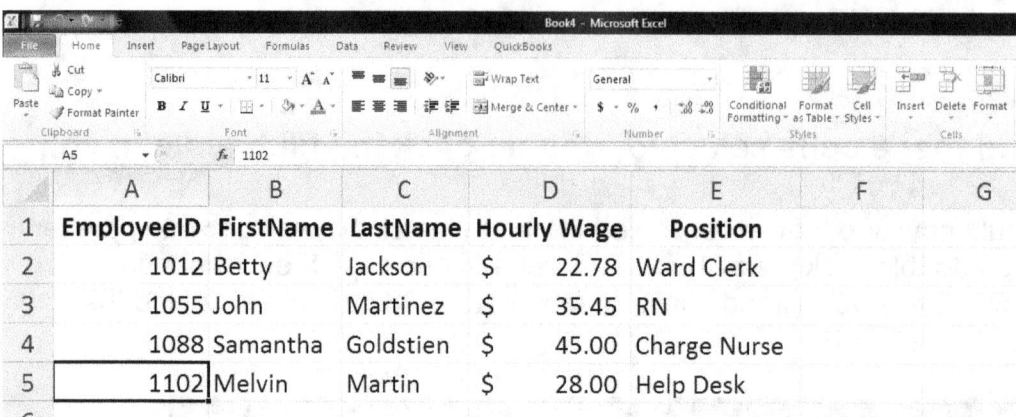

An Excel lookup table will consist of rows and columns, as shown above. The first column is the unique value you are looking up, an employee number or part number for example. This value could be a name or a number as long as it occurs only once in the first column. The values or labels in the first column must be sorted in ascending order for the Vlookup() function to work properly. The remaining columns are the values or fields associated with the ID number you are looking up. After creating the table of values, you can then use the Vlookup function to lookup the items in other columns tied to the looked up name or number.

For this portion of the exercise you will use the VLookup() function in a No Fault Travel workbook. In this scenario, you will assume that each No Fault Travel destination has a set cost per day when booking a trip. For instance, trips to Maui may always be $400 per day. If this is the case, you can construct a lookup table that has the destination and its associated cost per day. Then, using the Vlookup function, you could then type the destination in a workbook and Excel would then automatically display the cost per day, based on the look up table. This is exactly what you will do in this portion of the lesson.

The syntax for the Vlookup() function is as follows:

=*Vlookup(value to lookup, table that contains the list, column with the value you want)*

This syntax will make more sense after you have created a formula using this function.

1.   In a new workbook, move to Sheet3 and enter the data shown.

Excel 2010: Beyond The Basics

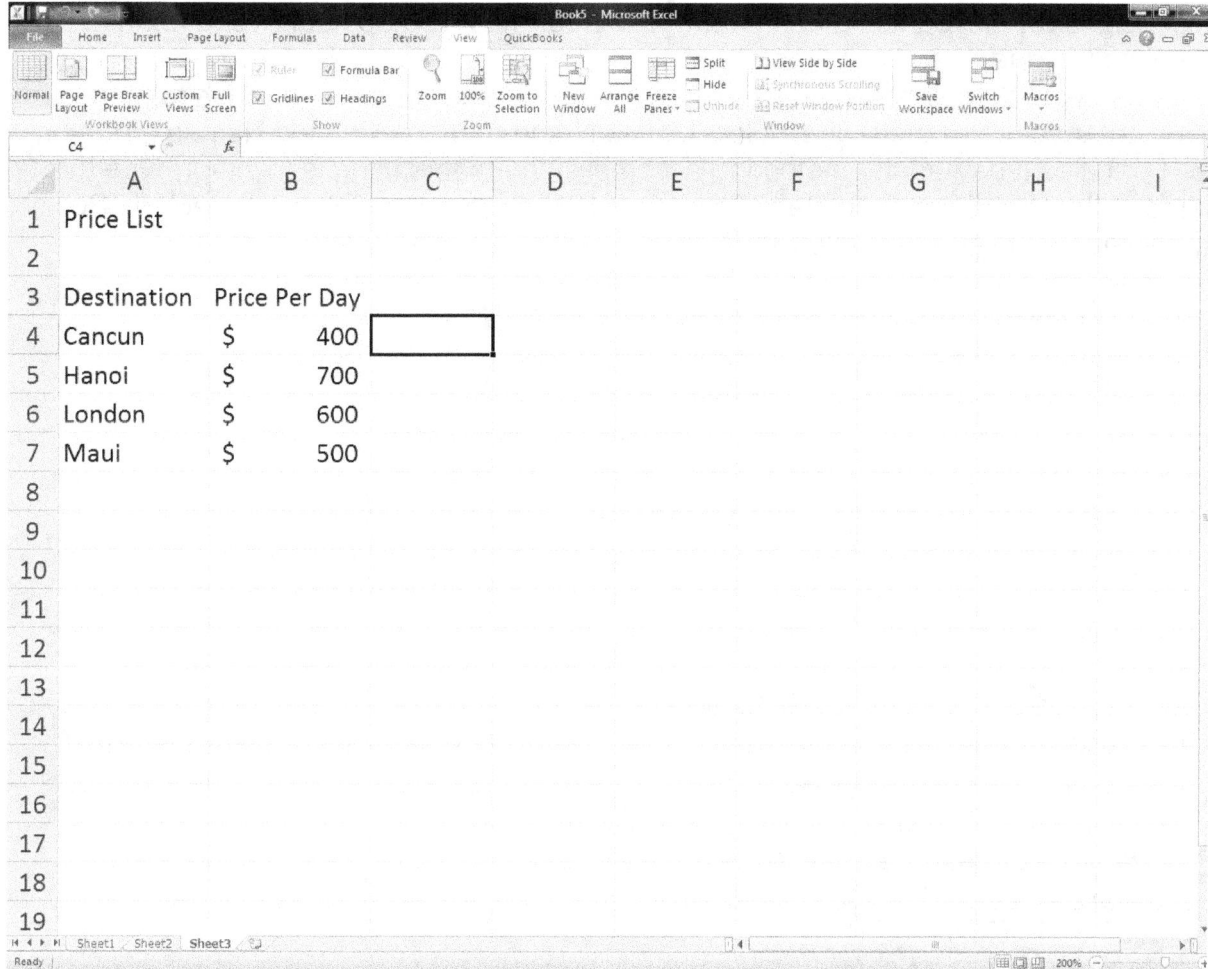

This is the table you will use with the Vlookup function. When creating a lookup table, the items in the leftmost column must be sorted numerically or alphabetically in ascending order.

2. Rename Sheet3, *Pricing*.
Remember, you can double-click the sheet tab to change a sheet's name.

Creating Named Ranges

Excel allows you to assign names to individual cells or ranges of cells. Naming a cell or range of cells often makes it easier to refer to them in formulas. For example, you will be using the price list you just created in several formulas. Naming this range PriceList, will allow you to refer to it by name rather than having to type Sheet1!A4:B7 each time you need it in a formula.

Another advantage to using Named Ranges is that Excel automatically adds absolute reference to named ranges. For example, if you create a Vlookup formula and want to copy that formula, you would have to ensure that the price list table was absolutely referenced, Sheet1!$A$4:b7. You would do this by manually adding the dollar signs ($). If you use a named range in a formula, you do not have to remember the absolute reference each time.

To name a cell or range of cells, first select the cell or cells you wish to name. Then, after selecting the range, select Define Name from the Defined Names group on the Formulas tab. A faster method to accomplish the same thing is to simply type the name in the Name Box to the left of the formula bar when the cells are selected. Be aware that Excel does not allow the use of spaces in range names.

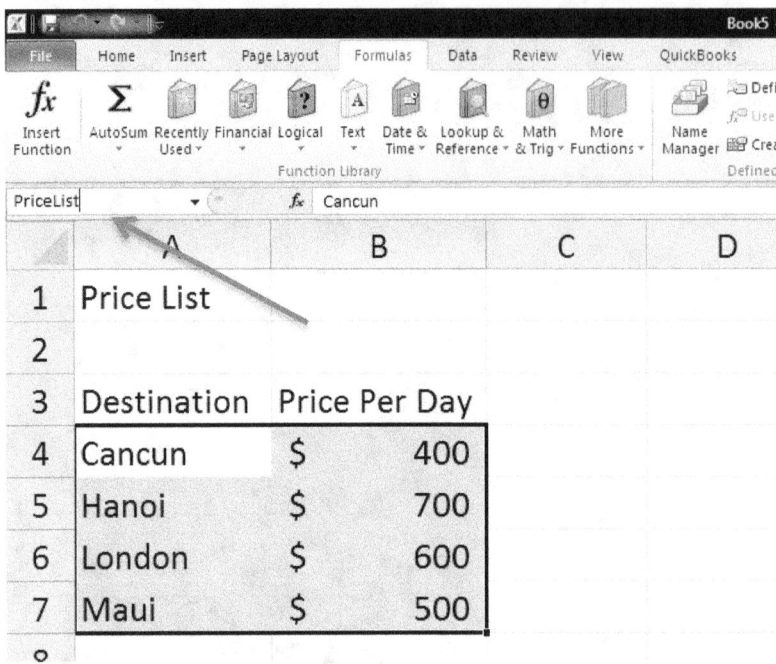

1. **In Sheet3 (Pricing), select cells A4:B7. Then, click in the Name Box and type *PriceList* as the name for this range and press (Enter).**

Do not add a space to the range name. Excel does not accept spaces in range names.

From this point on you can refer to Pricing!A4:B7 as PriceList in Excel formulas.

2. **Move to Sheet1 and change this sheet's name to *January*.**

Naming a sheet is not the same as naming a range of cells, but as you saw in a previous lesson, it also makes formulas easier to create.

Excel 2010: Beyond The Basics

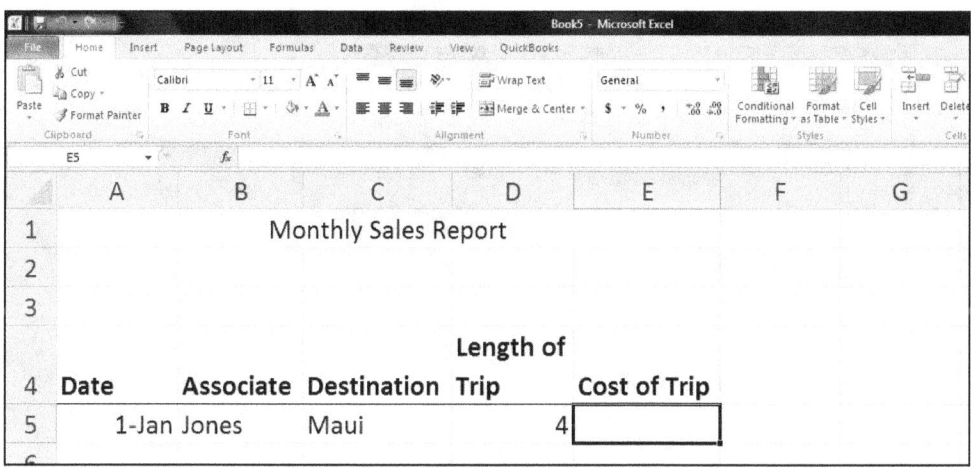

3. **In the January worksheet, enter the data shown above.**
To have cell D4, Length of Trip, appear as shown you will need to turn on the Wrap Text option (Home tab, Alignment, Wrap Text) for this cell. Depending on when you selected this option, you may also need to adjust the height of the cell to have it fit properly.

You are now ready to create a formula that calculates the cost of the trip. To do this you will look up the cost per day for Maui and multiply that cost by the trip length. You will use the Vlookup() function to create this formula.

4. **Move to cell E5 and begin the formula by typing =*Vlookup(C5* and then typing a comma (,).**

The first argument in the Vlookup function is the value you are looking up in the table (C5). In this example, you are looking up the price for Maui. The comma (,) separates the arguments.

5. **Continue the formula by typing *PriceList* and then a comma (,).**
The next argument is the table that contains the value you are looking up and the value you want in this cell. You are using the range name to make creating this formula easier.

6. **Complete the formula by typing *2)* and pressing (Enter).**
The last argument is the column that contains the value you want in this cell. This table has two columns. The price per day is in column two. Lookup tables may have several columns if you needed to lookup up more than one value based on the destination.

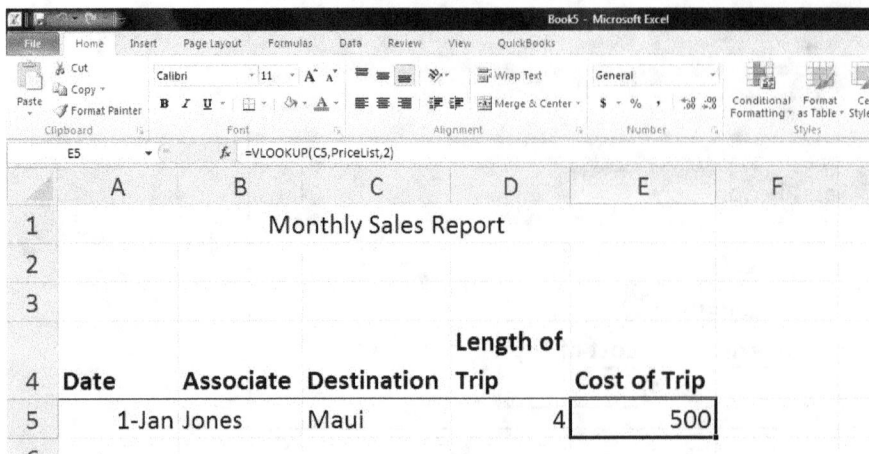

You should now see that Excel looked up the price per day for Maui. You now need to edit the formula so that it multiplies this cost by the trip length.

7. Move back into cell E5 and edit the Vlookup() formula so that the value it looks up is multiplied by cell D5.

You now will see the cost of the entire trip based on the value from the Price List table and the trip length.

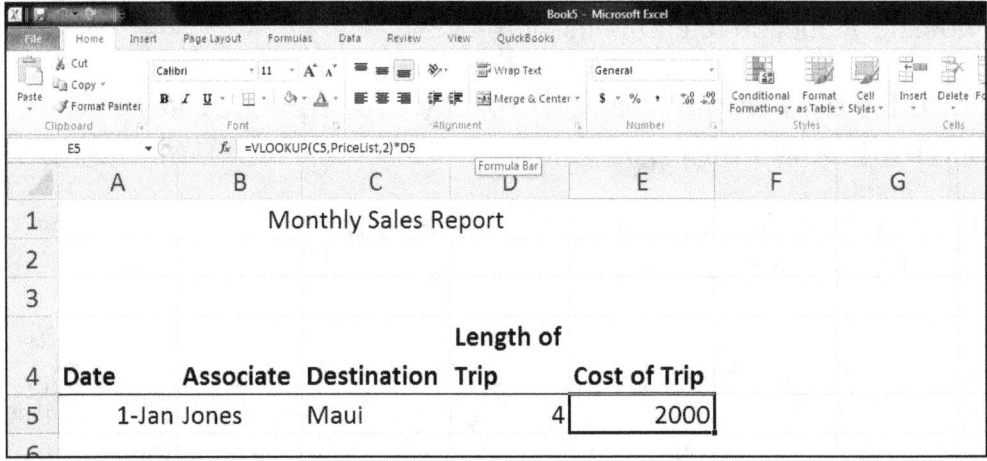

8. Copy the formula in cell E5 through cell E14.

You will see an error message in the empty rows. This is because there is nothing Excel can look up in the table in the empty rows. Ignore the error messages for now.

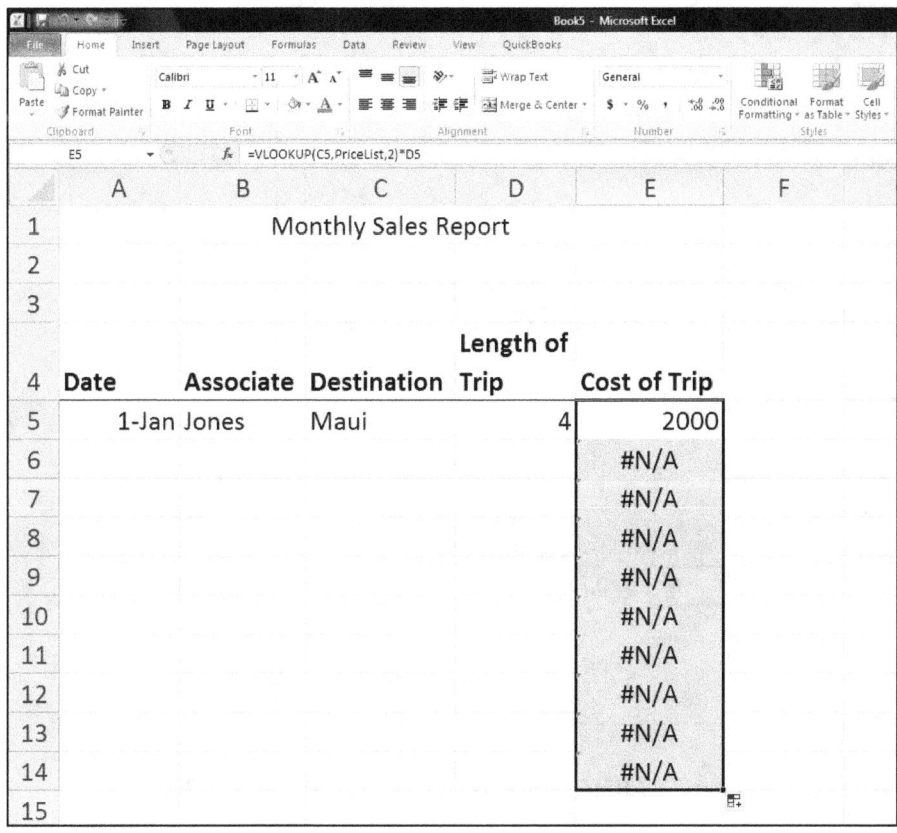

9. **Enter the additional information as shown. Verify that the Vlookup is working for each new entry.**

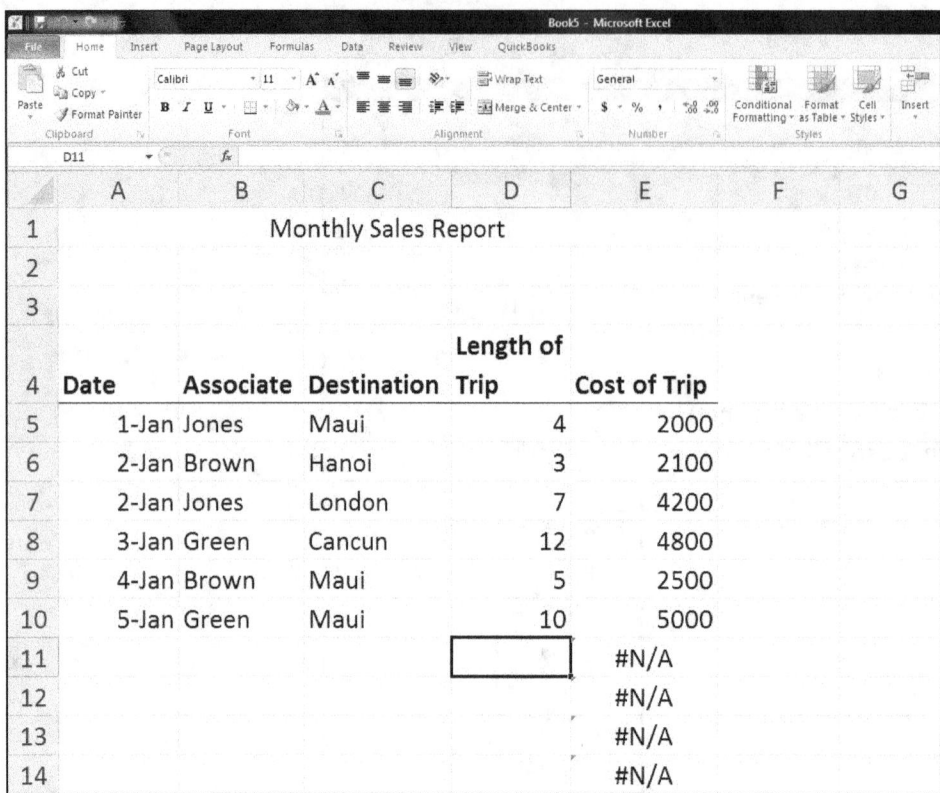

10. **Save this workbook as *Monthly Report* but leave it open.**

The IF() Function

The IF() function allows you to create formulas that compute differing values depending upon a condition. For example, assume that No Fault Travel gives a 5% discount if the total cost of the trip exceeds $2,500. To compute the discount, the formula will have to evaluate the cost of the trip. If the trip costs more than $2,500 then Excel should compute a discount. If the trip does not exceed $2,500 then the customer receives no discount.

The syntax of the IF() function is rather simple: =If(Condition to check, computation to perform if condition is true, computation to perform if condition is false).

In this portion of the lesson you will use the IF() function to compute a customer's discount based on the cost of the trip.

1. **In the Monthly Report workbook, move to cell F4, type *Discount* and then press (Enter).**

In cell F5 you will enter a formula using the IF() function.

Excel 2010: Beyond The Basics

2. **In cell F5 type the following formula:** =IF(E5>2500,E5*0.05,0)

   This computes a 5% discount on the total trip if the trip exceeds $2,500. If not, no discount is computed.

3. **Copy the formula from F5 through F14.**

   You may try double-clicking on the fill handle to quickly copy.

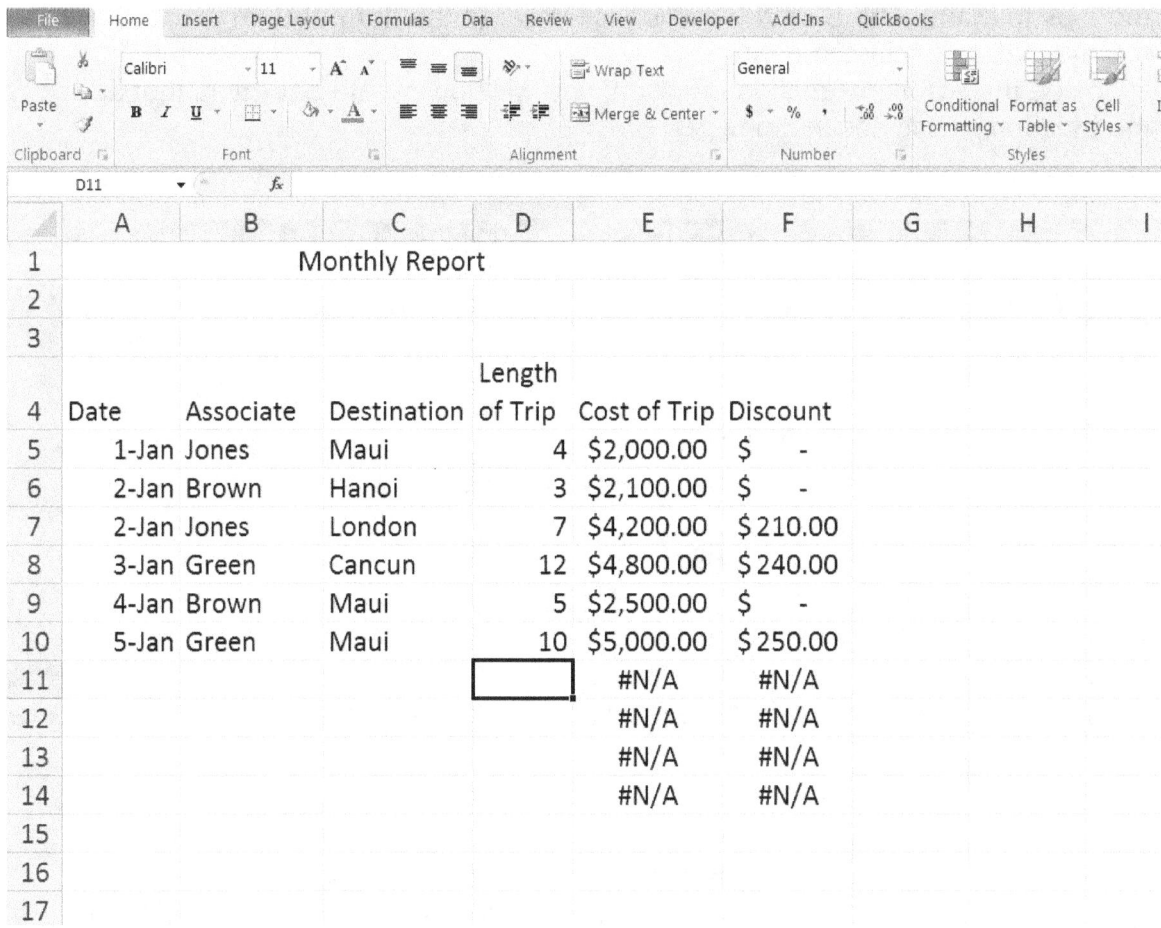

Nested If statements

It is possible to nest more than one If() functions in the same formula to make more than two possible outcomes. For example, if you wanted larger trip costs to qualify for a larger discount, you could enter a formula such as:

=IF(E5>5000,E5*0.08, IF(E5>2500,E5*.05,0))

In this example, a trip cost in cell E5 gets an 8% discount if it is over $5,000. If the trip is more than $2,500 but less than $5,001, it gets a 5% discount. If the trip costs $2,500 or less, it gets no discount. The number of If statements that you can include in a formula is limited. You can enter, or nest, no more than 64 levels of functions within a function. But, getting to that point makes for very complicated formulas.

Conditional summing: SumIf()

In addition to the If() function that stands alone, Excel also offers a few conditional statistics such as SumIf(), AverageIf(), and CountIf(). These functions combine their normal function with a condition. For example, if you wanted to know the total of all the trips to Maui, you could use the SumIf() function. This function would sum only the trips to Maui. The SumIf() function is similar to the normal Sum function except that you must also specify the condition.

To see the SUMIF() function in action, you will now create a formula that adds only the trips to specific destinations.

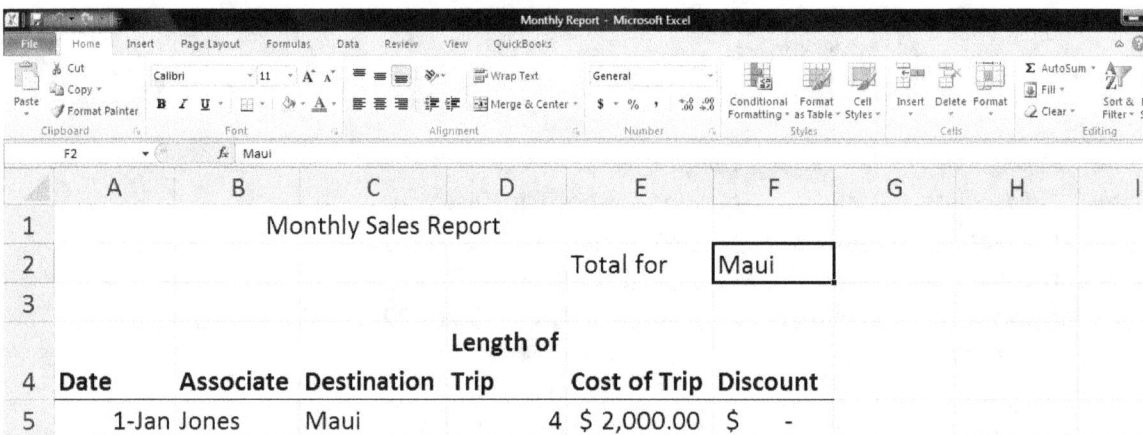

1. **Move to cell E2 and type *Total for* and then move (Right) to move to cell F2.**

2. **In cell F2 type *Maui* and move (Right).**

   You are placing Maui in a separate cell because this will be the condition you want Excel to use to Sum the trips. Placing the condition in a separate cell will also allow you to change the destination and then see the sum for whatever destination you type in cell F2.

3. **Move to cell G2 and begin a formula by clicking the Insert Function tool at the left edge of the formula bar.**

4. **Locate the SUMIF function and click OK.**
You can find this function in the Math & Trig category.

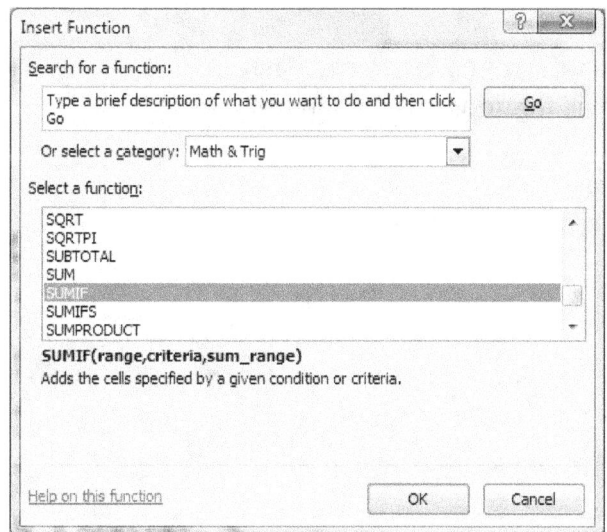

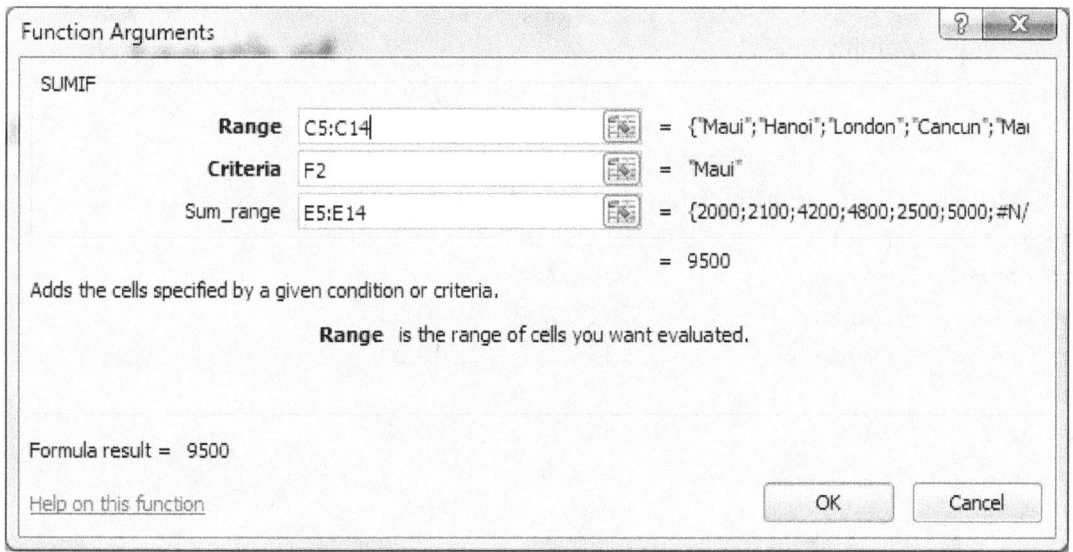

You should now see the Function Arguments dialog box which will help you build this formula.

5. **In the Range text box type or select C5:C14.**
This is the range where you want Excel to look for the value you are basing the condition on, in other words Maui.

6. **In the Criteria text box type or click on cell F2.**
The criteria is the cell where you will type the destination you want to total the trips for.

7. **In the Sum Range type or select cells E5:E14.**
   The sum range contains the values you want summed, in this case the cost of the trips.

8. **Click OK after entering the correct parameters.**
   You should now see the total of all the trips to Maui in cell G2.

9. **Change cell F2 to read *London*.**
   Notice the sum changes as the criteria value changes.

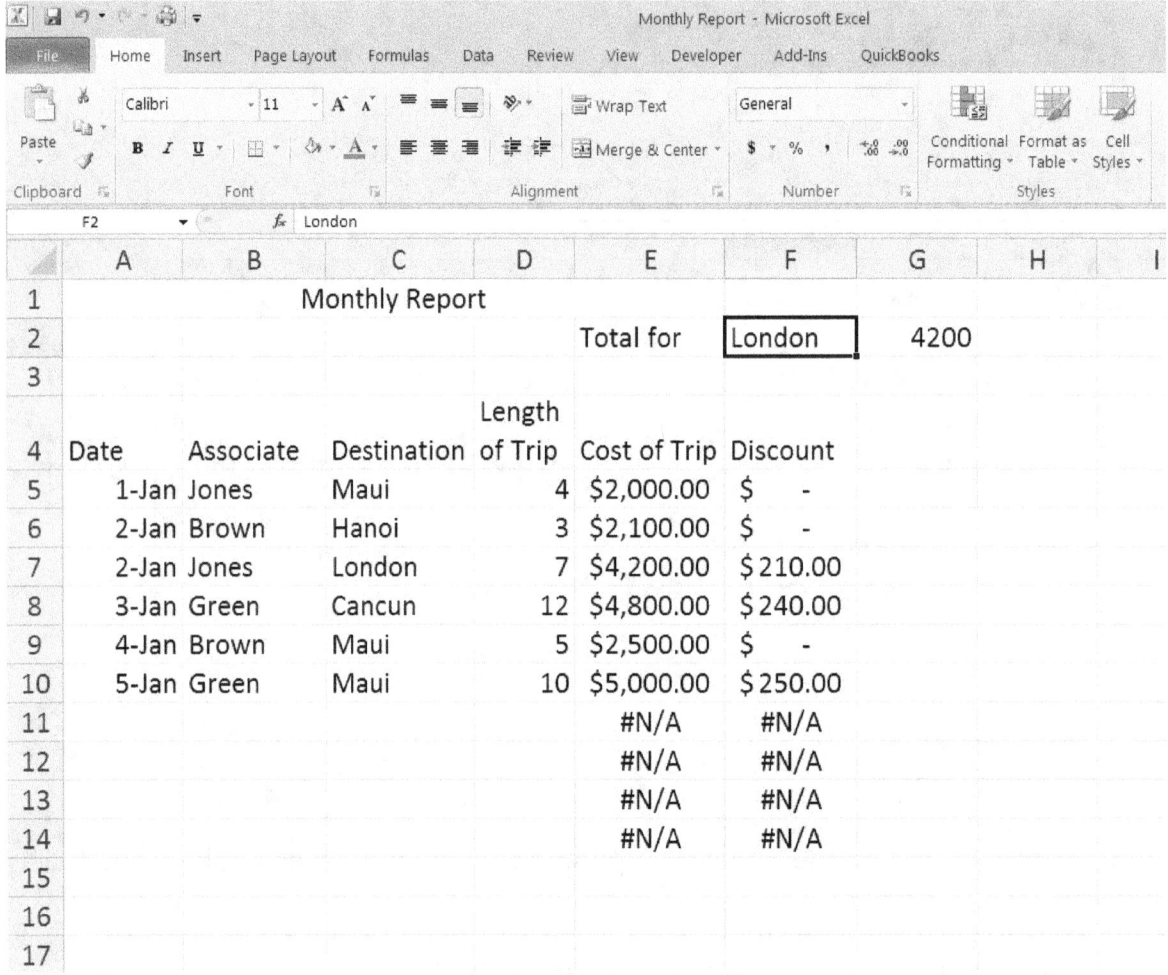

10. **Save and close the workbook.**

Skill Builder: Lesson #3

In this skill builder you will use the IF() function to enter words into cells rather than values. First you will add a Spent column to the monthly budget worksheet. Then, you will create an over/under column that will display the words "Over Budget" or "Within Budget" based on whether the amount spent was less than or greater than the amount budgeted.

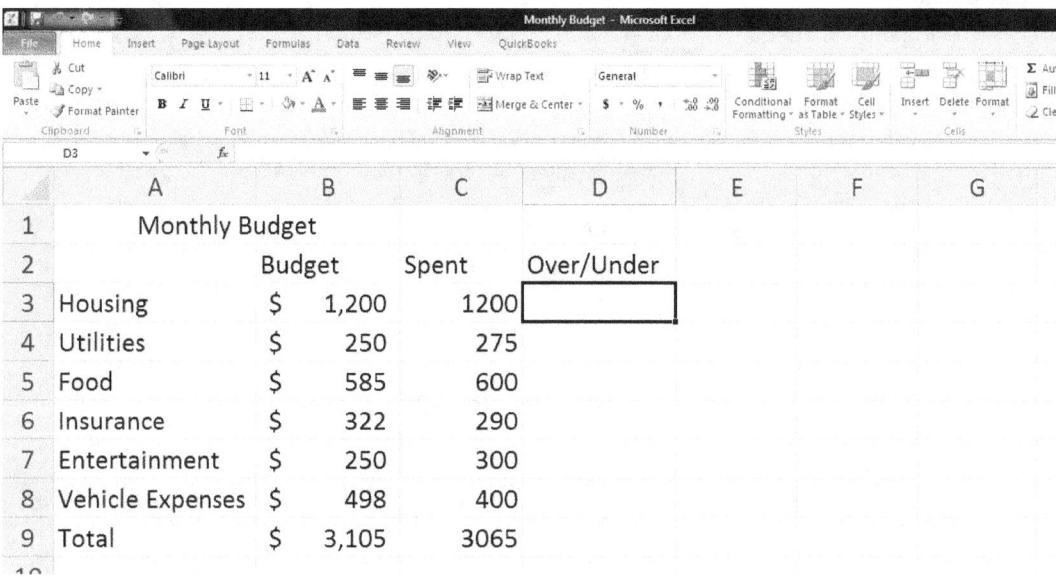

1. Open the Monthly Budget workbook and add the labels and values shown on the January worksheet.

2. Create a formula in cell D3 that compares the difference between the amounts budgeted and spent. If the amount spent is greater than the amount budgeted, the formula should display "Over Budget". If the amount is not over, the formula should display "Within Budget".

   Hint: When using words rather than computations in IF() functions, the words need to be enclosed in quotation marks.

   Try your best, but if you need help, the correct formula is shown in the formula bar in the image on the next page.

Excel 2010: Beyond The Basics

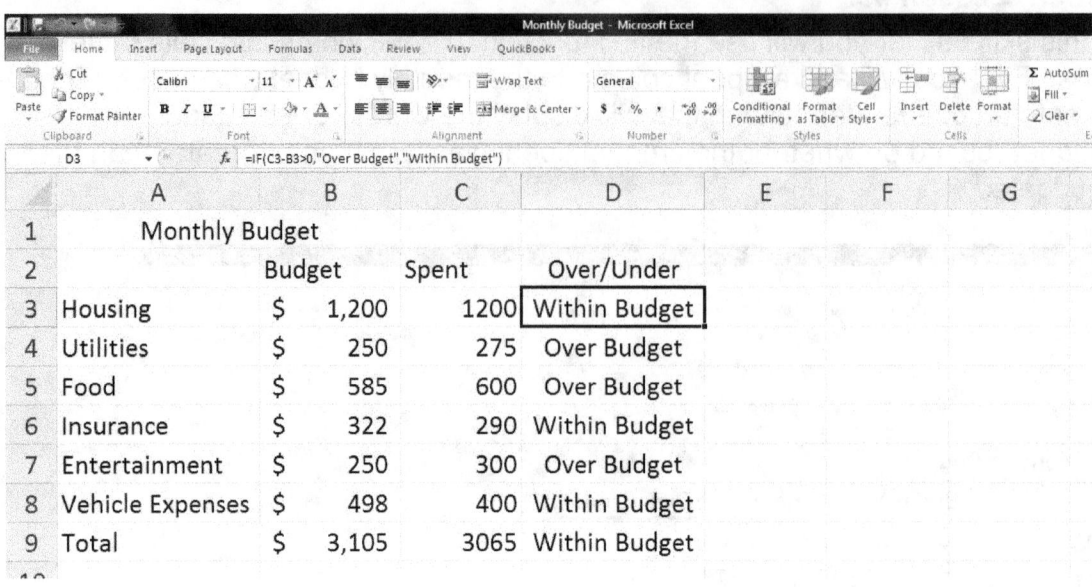

3. **Save and close the workbook when done.**

Lesson #4: Additional Graphing Features

In this lesson you will learn to:
- *Add Data to charts*
- *Combine chart types*
- *Add graphic elements to charts*

Lesson #4: Enhancing Excel Charts

It is very easy to create charts and graphs based on the values in an Excel workbook. To create a simple chart you simply select the cells you want to include in the chart and then insert the chart.

In this lesson you will explore some additional features available within Excel charts. You will learn to add additional data series to a chart, create a combination chart, use a secondary axis, as well as some additional annotating and formatting features. To explore these additional charting features you will use the *Travel Report* workbook you created in Lesson #2. You will begin by creating a column chart that displays the total for each salesperson for the month of January. After that, you will add the additional month's data.

1. **Open *Travel Report* and go to the *January* worksheet.**

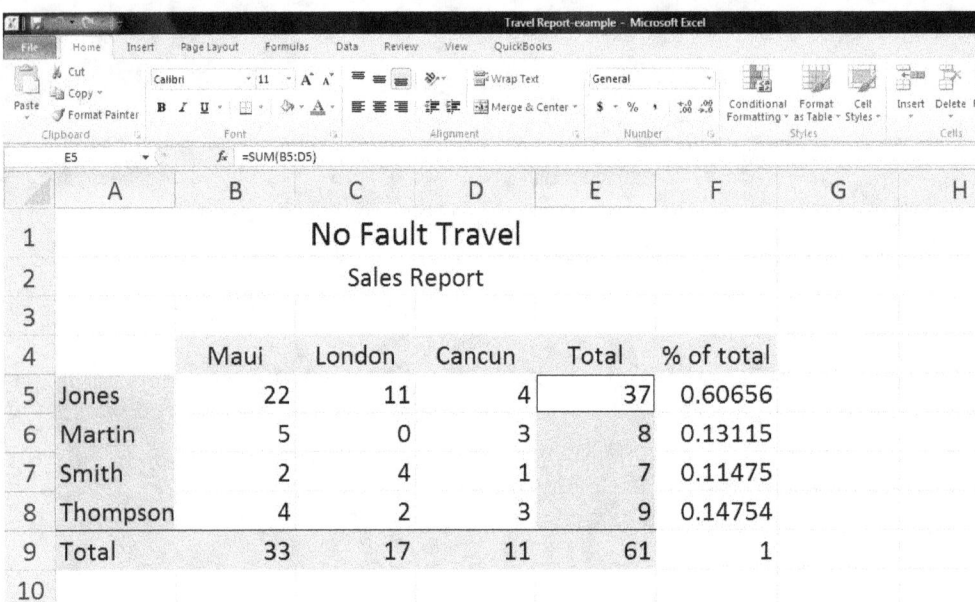

2. **On the January worksheet, select cells A5:A8 and E5:E8.**
You have selected the data you want Excel to chart, the names of each salesperson and the total for that month.
Remember, you can use the (Control) key to select non-contiguous ranges.

Excel 2010: Beyond The Basics

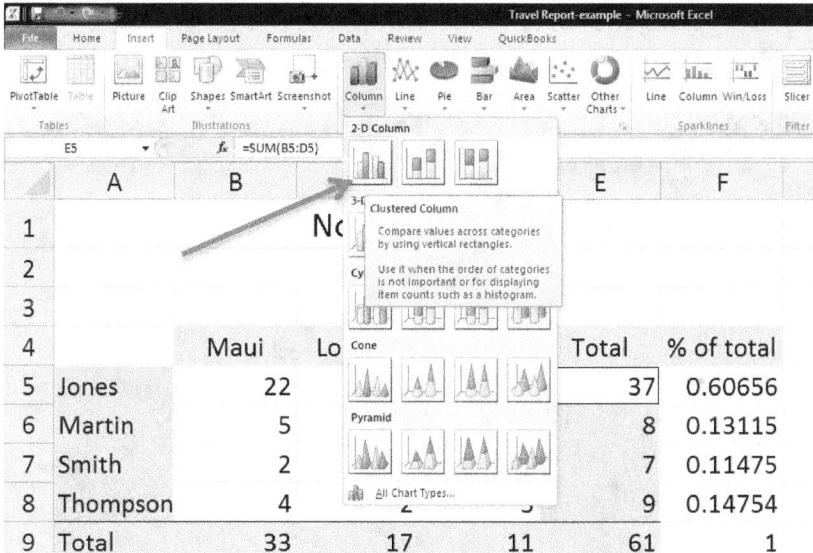

3. Choose the Column chart tool on the Insert ribbon. Select the Clustered 2-d column chart as shown.

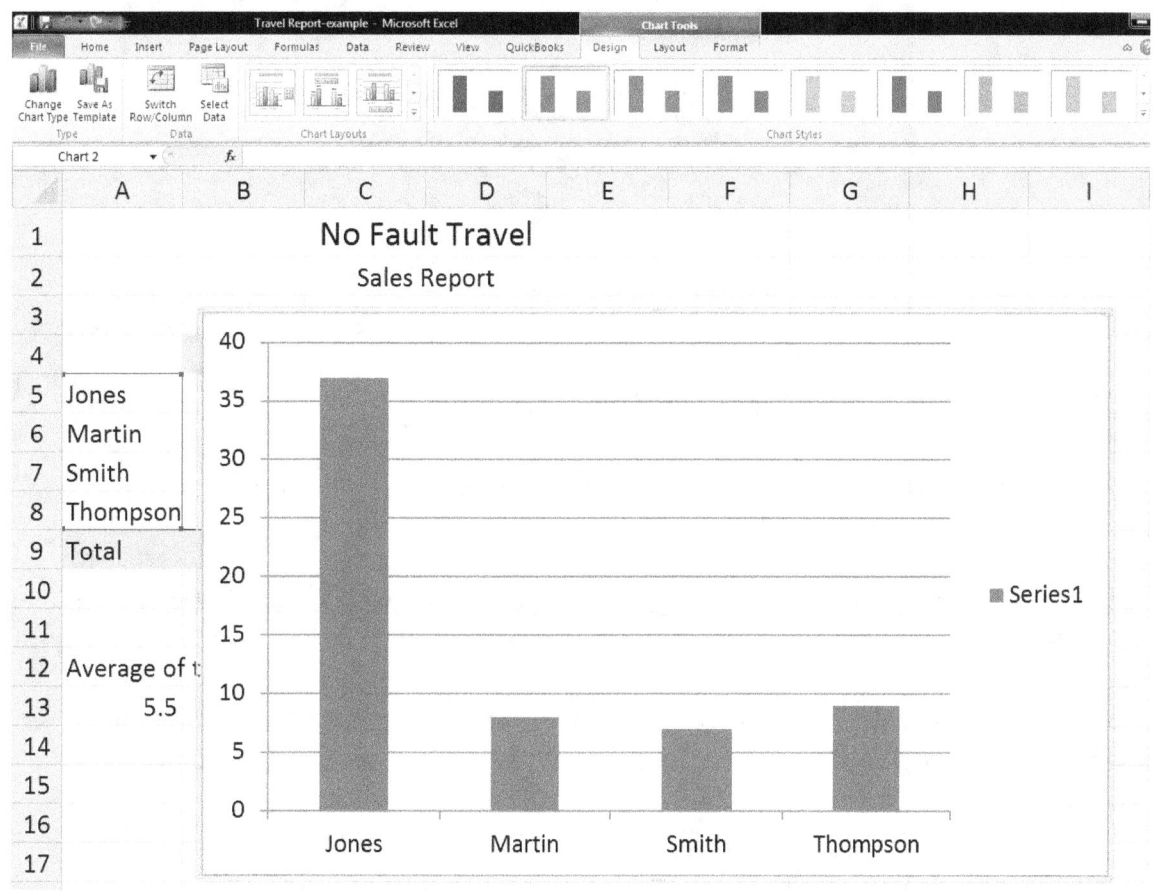

Excel places the column chart over the data in the worksheet. You will now move this chart to a new worksheet.

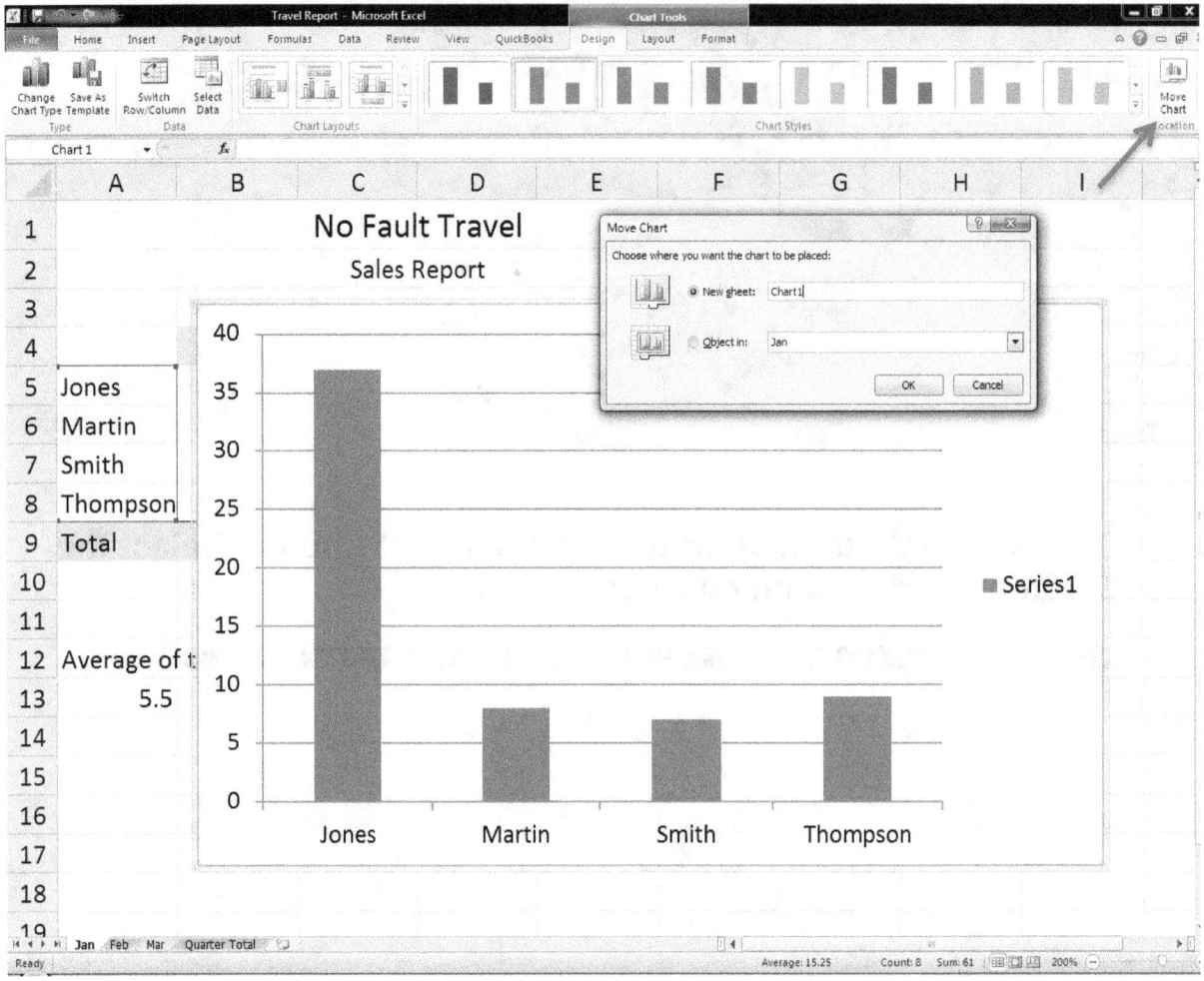

4. Click the Move Chart tool in the Location group on the Design Tab.

Excel will then display the Move Chart dialog box. Here you will instruct Excel to move this chart to a separate worksheet.

5. In the Move Chart dialog box, select the New sheet option and click OK.

Your chart will now be in a separate worksheet and will not interfere with the worksheet data. Now you will add the other month's data to this chart but using the Select Data tool.

Excel 2010: Beyond The Basics

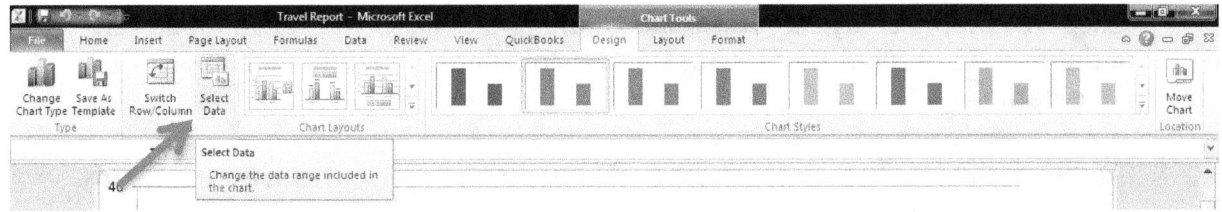

6. Make sure you are viewing the chart, then click the Select Data tool on the Design Tab.

Adding and editing data series

Excel now displays the Select Data Source dialog box. This dialog box allows you to add additional data series to the chart. It also allows you to change the name of the data series. For example, right now your chart displays "Series 1" in the legend. After adding the other months, you will have Excel display the month name of each series in the legend.

To add more data to the chart you will use the Add button in this dialog box. To edit the series, such as to change the data the current series is charting or to change the name of the data series, you will use the Edit tool. In this lesson you will start with the Edit tool to change the name of the first data series.

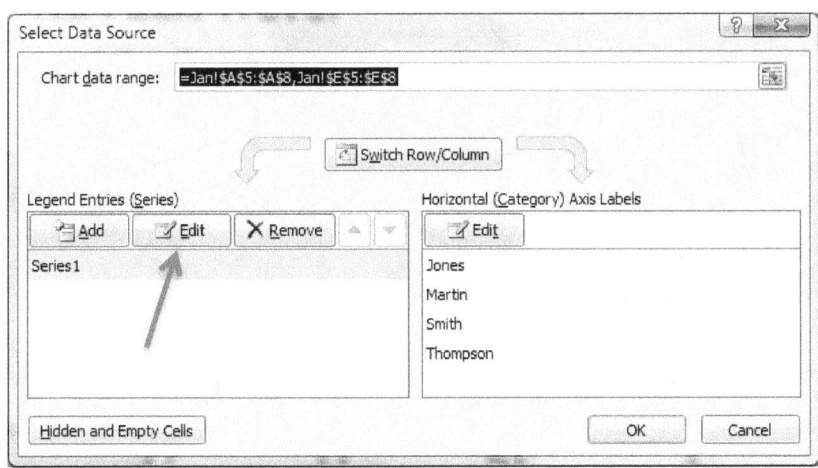

1. In the Select Data Source dialog box, click the Edit button.

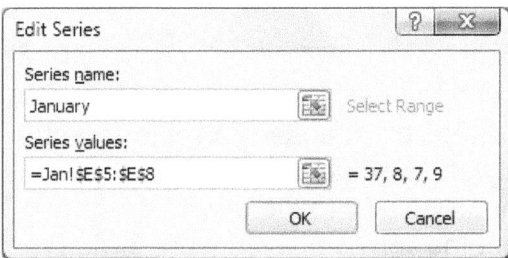

Excel will then display the Edit Series dialog box. Here you can change the name of data series or alter the cells included in this series on the chart. You will change the name.

2. **In the Edit Series dialog box, type *January* in the Series name text area and click OK.**

The Select Data Source dialog box should remain open. Do not close it.

If you look at the legend of the chart, you should notice that Excel now displays January in the legend rather than *Series1*. You will now add data series for February and March so the chart includes all three months.

3. **Click the Add button in the Select Data Source dialog box.**

Excel displays the Edit Series dialog box, even though you are adding new data to the chart. You should notice that the Series name and Series values text areas contain no meaningful data. To add more data to the chart you will enter the series name and select the data to include in the chart.

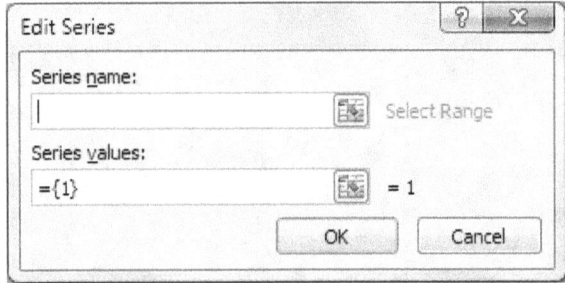

4. **Type *February* in the Series name text area and press the (Tab) key.**

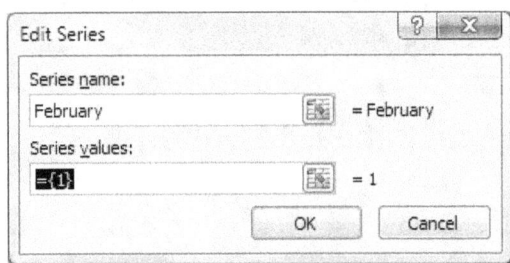

Pressing Tab to move to the next field in this dialog box caused Excel to select the ={1} in the series value text area. To successfully add another data series, this entry must be erased before selecting the cells you want to add to the chart. If this text is not selected, erase it manually. Now you will select the next cells you want to add to the graph.

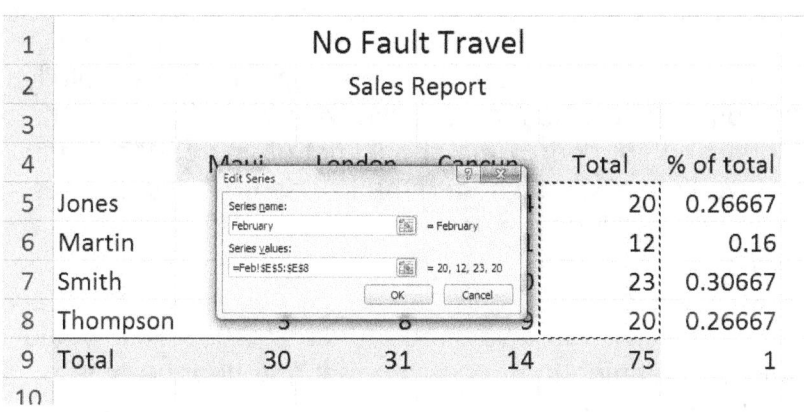

5. Click on the February worksheet, select cells E5 through E8 and click OK.

As you examine the chart you should notice that Excel has added another column that displays February's totals for each salesperson.

6. Click the Add button again and repeat the process to add the totals from the March worksheet to the chart. Close the Select Data Source dialog box when done.

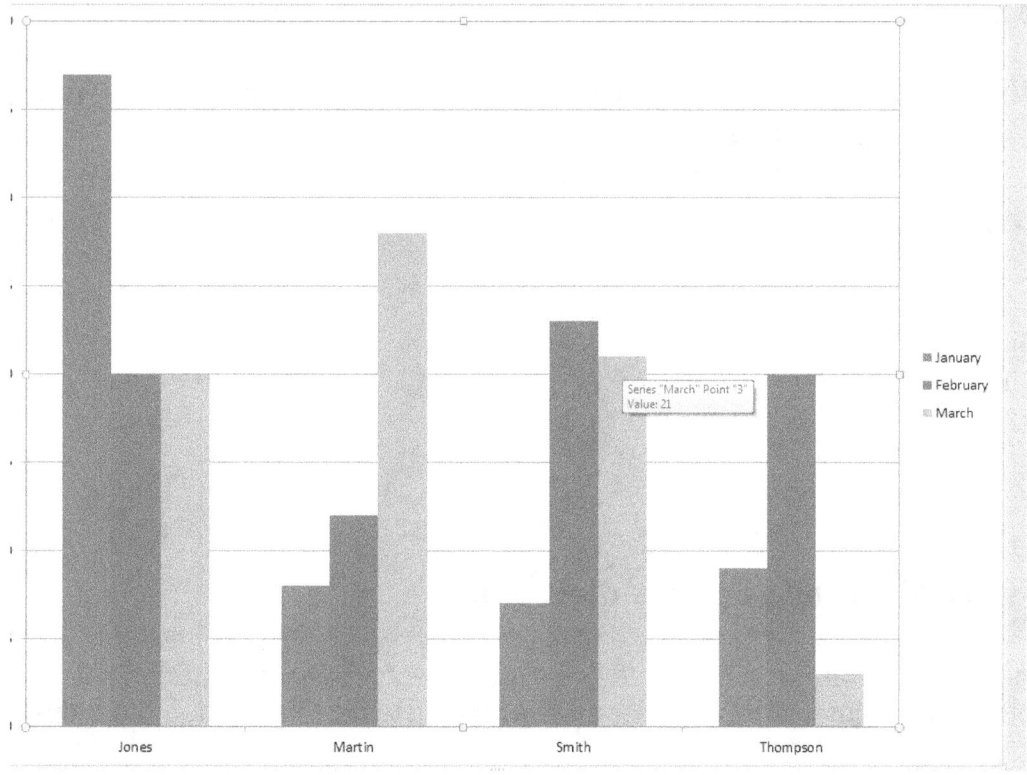

Your chart should appear similar to that above. It should have all three months displayed in the legend and in the chart itself.

Combining Chart types

When you create a chart you should choose the data that appears on it carefully. Sometimes it is best to create two different charts than to have widely varying data on the same chart. For example, detail and summary data should not often appear on the same chart. In this Travel Report worksheet, if you added the values from the Quarter Total worksheet to this chart, Excel would adjust the scale of the value (Y) axis to accommodate the larger numbers.

Currently the value axis displays a top value close to 40. By adding the summary data to the chart, the top value would increase to a value approaching 100. This would cause the monthly columns to shrink in relation to the column that graphed the enter total for the person. Combining both types of data, summary and detail, causes a loss of visual accuracy for the detail data.

Even though it is often best to create two separate charts, in some cases it is necessary to display both summary and detail data on the same chart. In these situations Excel allows you to combine different chart types, essentially displaying two separate charts on the same worksheet. For example, you may have a chart that has some data series charted with columns and another with a line chart. This is especially useful when the series vary greatly in value, such as the Travel Report's totals and monthly data. It is also possible to have two separate value (Y) axes which allows for easier visual interpretation of both the summary and detail data.

In this portion of the lesson you will add a data series that charts the totals for all three months for each destination. You will then change the chart type for this data series and add another value axis to the chart.

1. **Click the Select Data tool on the Design tab. Then, click the Add button in the Select Data Source dialog box. Name the new series *Total* and add cells B5 though B8 on the Quarter Total worksheet.**

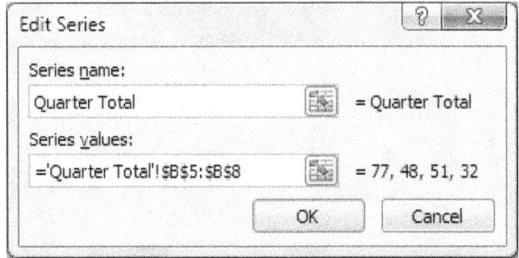

2. **Close the Select Data Source dialog box.**

You should notice that Excel added the totals to the chart and adjusted the Y axis. The monthly total columns now appear smaller because Excel adjusted the value axis.

You will now change the chart type to Line for the Quarter Totals and create a secondary value axis.

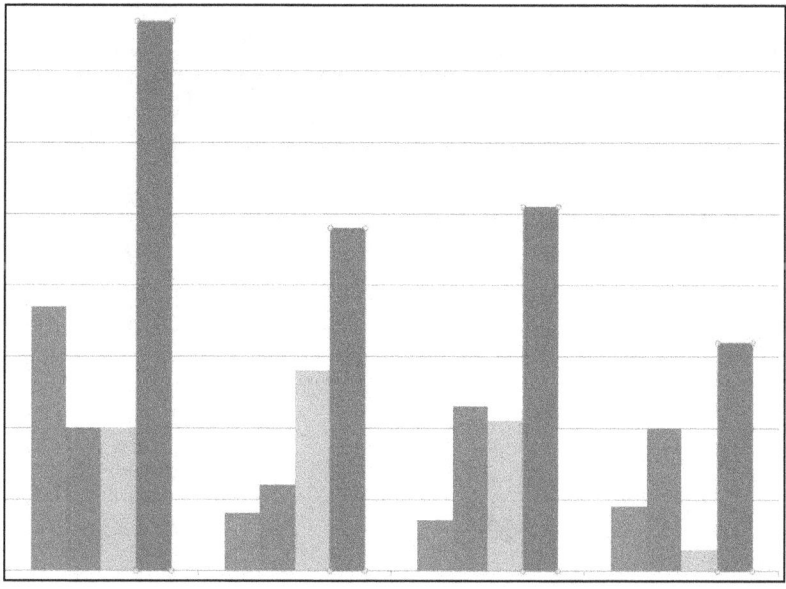

3. Carefully click on any of the total columns to select the entire series.

All four of the Quarter Total columns should have sizing handles at the top and bottom when they are selected. If only one column is selected, click in a blank area of the chart and try again. You will now change the chart type to Line. But, because only this series is selected, only the Quarter Totals will change to a line chart.

4. Click the Change Chart Type tool on the Design tab.

Excel should now display the Change Chart Type dialog box.

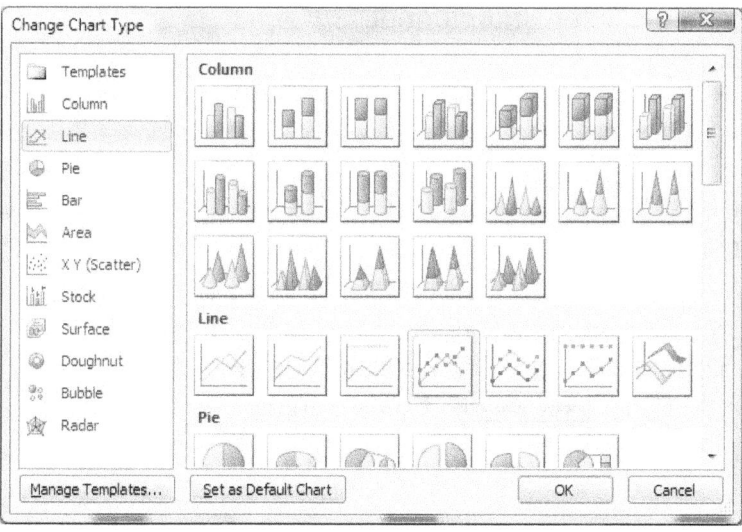

5. In the Change Chart Type click Line and click OK.

Excel 2010: Beyond The Basics

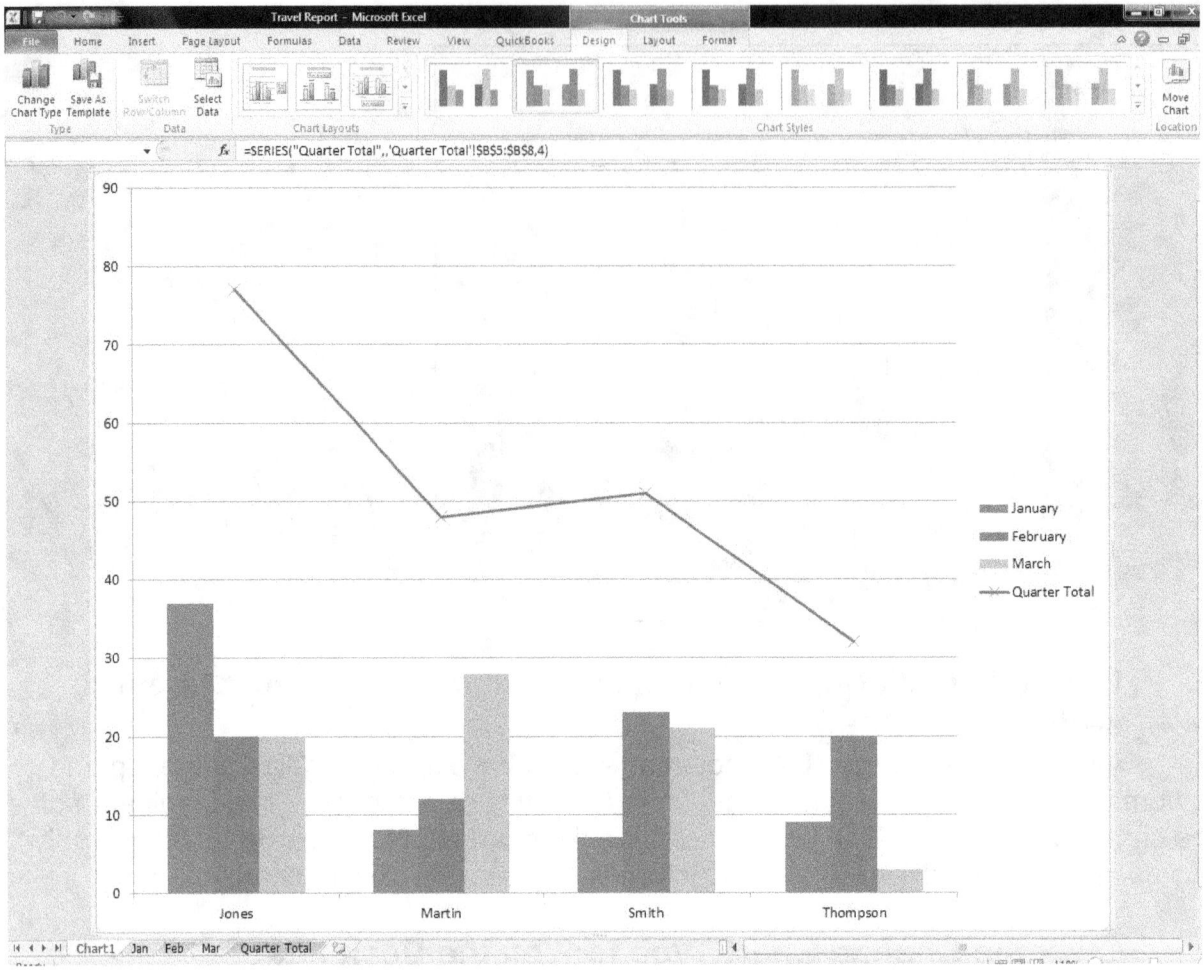

Excel has now changed the chart type for the Quarter Total series to Line. The monthly totals should still be displayed in column chart format.

The value (Y) axis did not change when you changed the chart type. You will now add a second value axis to this chart.

6. **Click in a blank area of the chart and then on the line in the chart to select this data series.**

You should notice sizing handles on each data point in the line. This lets you know the entire series is selected. You will now use the Format Data Series command to inform Excel you want to use a secondary axis with this data series.

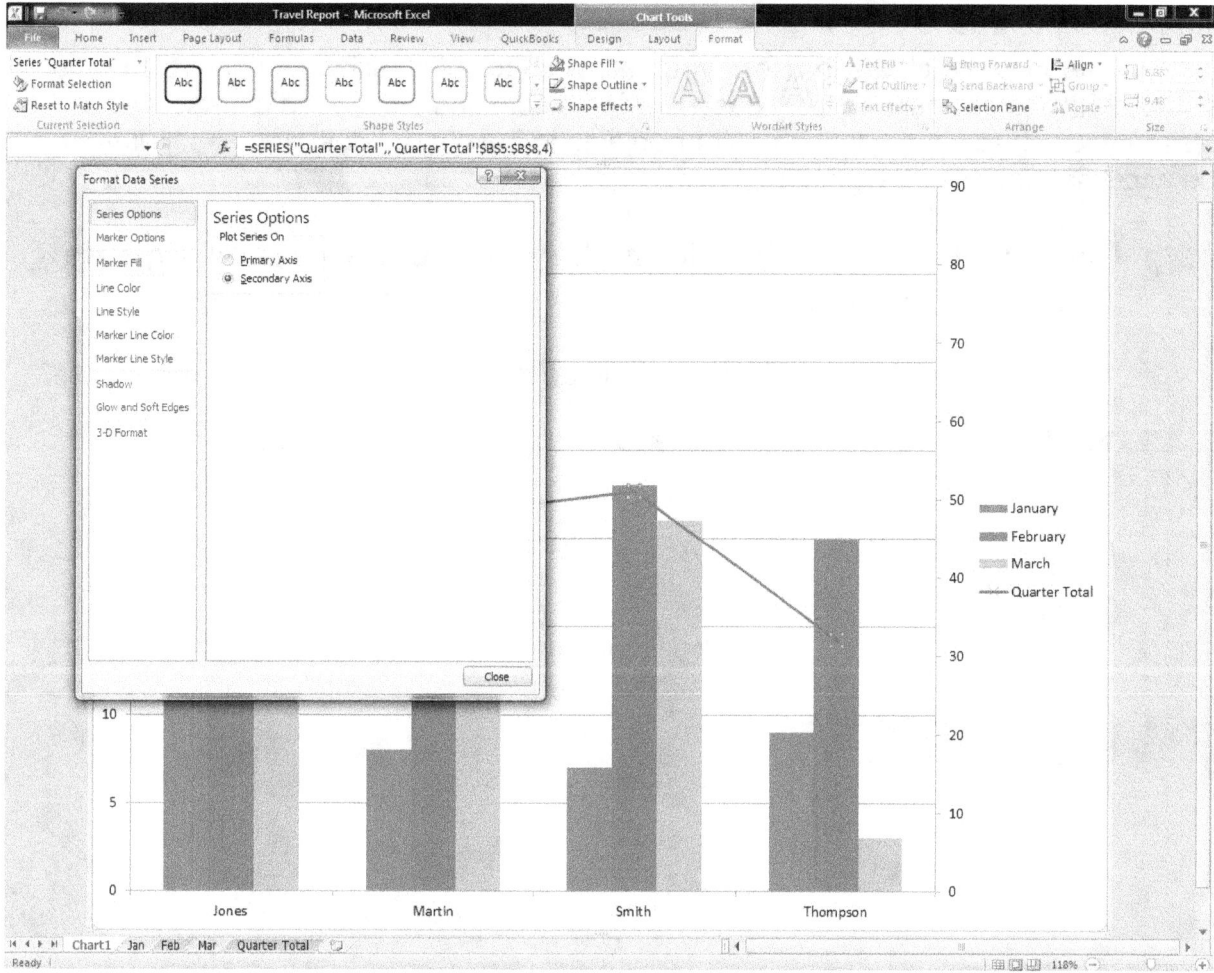

7. **Click the Format Selection tool in the Format tab to display the Format Data Series dialog box.**

8. **In the Format Data Series dialog box, click the Secondary Axis radio button and click Close.**

   As you return to your chart you should notice that Excel added a secondary axis that it uses for the Quarter Totals series. It also adjusted the primary value axis to fit the monthly totals.

Excel 2010: Beyond The Basics

Annotating charts

After creating charts in Excel, you may want to call special attention to a portion of the chart. Excel makes it very easy to add objects and pictures to charts. In this lesson you will add some text and other objects to the chart. Most of these features can be accessed from the Layout tab.

1. Click the Chart Title tool in the Layout tab in the Labels group and add a title of *Sales by Salesperson* above the chart.

After adding a title, you will now add an arrow and a text box to the chart.

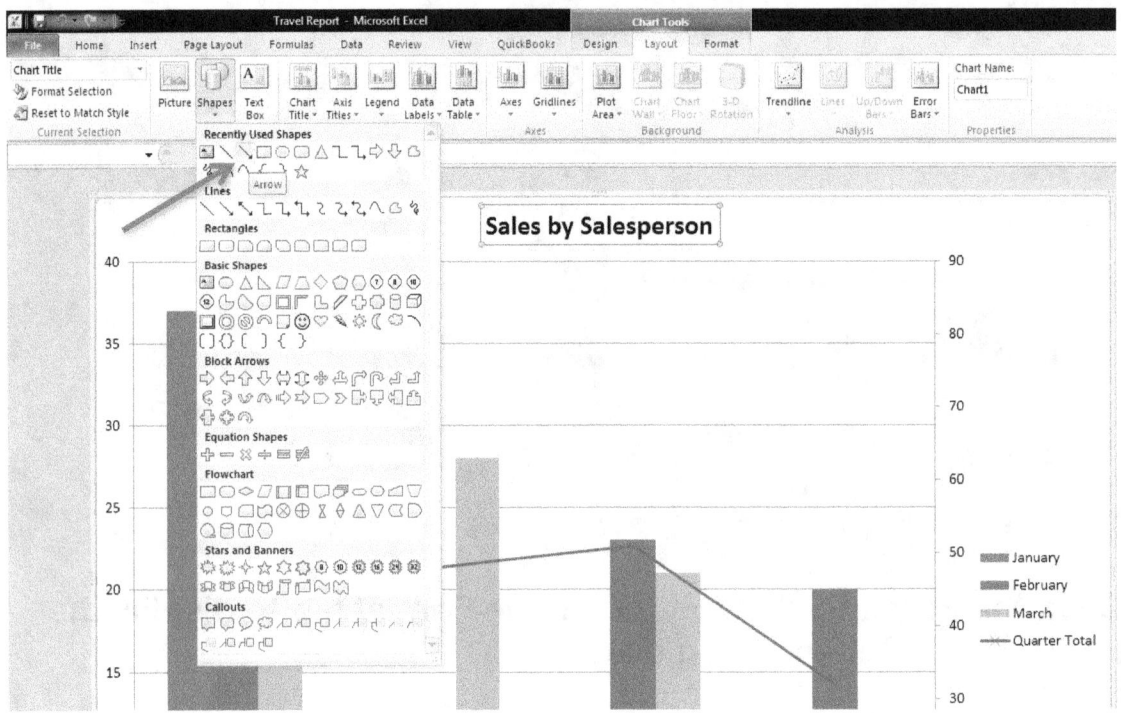

2. Click the Shapes tool on the Layout tool and select the Arrow shape.

The arrow tool is similar to the line tool except that one end of the line will have an arrow tip. Changes to the arrow may be made from the Shape Styles group.

© 2014 Luther M. Maddy III

Excel 2010: Beyond The Basics

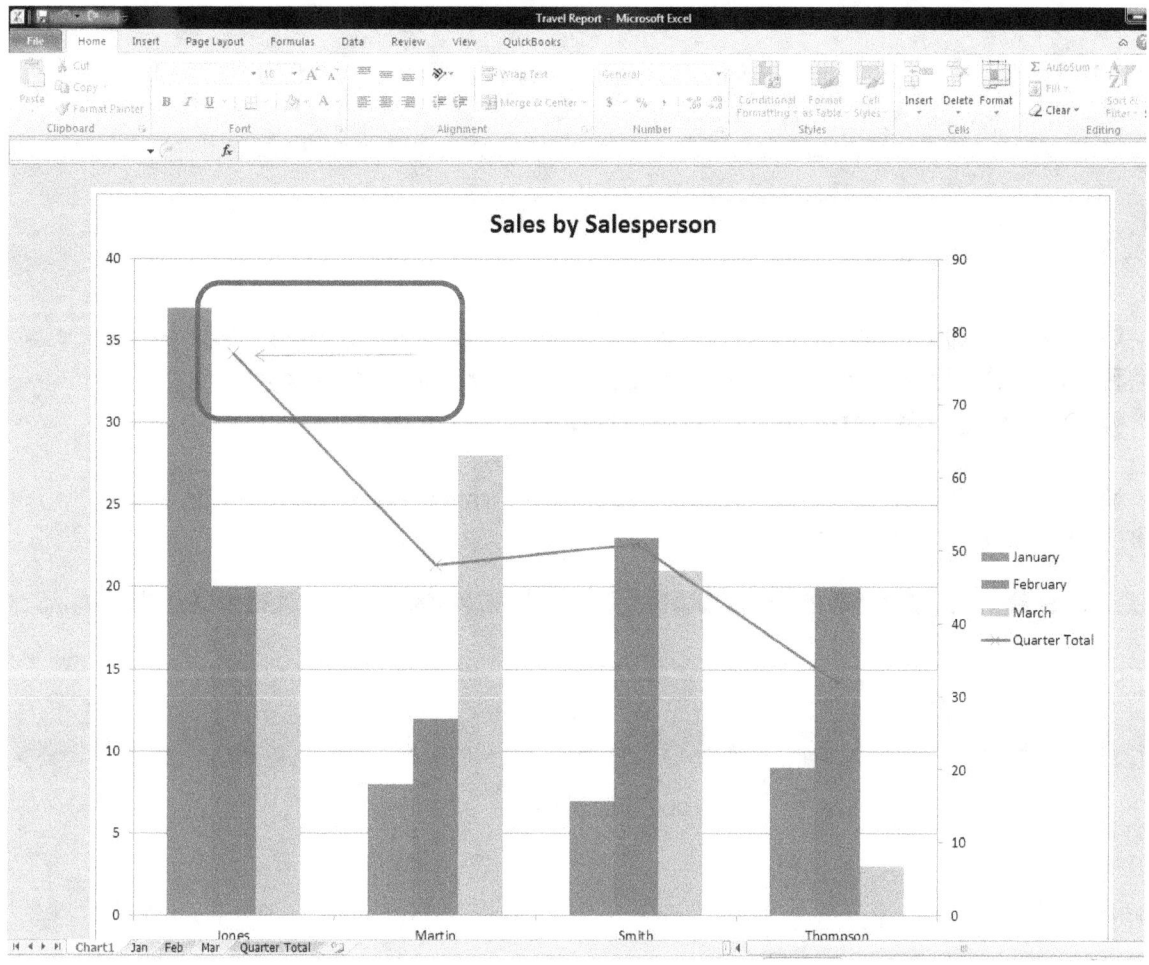

3. **Click and drag to draw the arrow as shown, pointing to the total for Jones.**

The arrow will appear where your mouse point is when you release the mouse. So, to have the arrow pointing left as shown, drag from right to left. After drawing the arrow you will change its appearance to make it thicker.

4. **Make sure the arrow you just drew is selected.**

You will see sizing circles at each end of the arrow when it is selected.

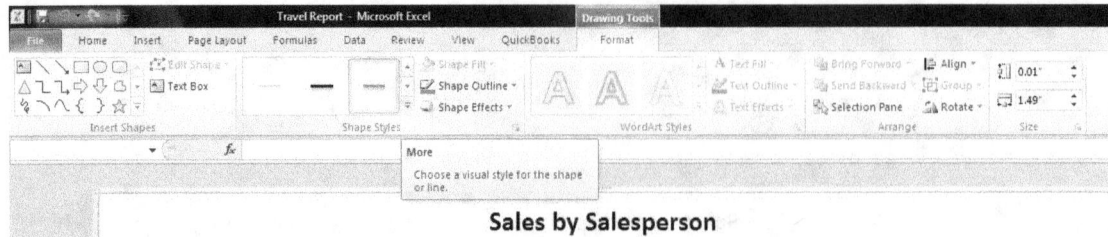

5. **Click the More drop down arrow for the line styles tool in the Shape Styles group and choose an arrow in the second row from the top to increase the arrow's thickness.**

Next, you will add a textbox at the end of the arrow. You will use this textbox to explain the arrow you just added.

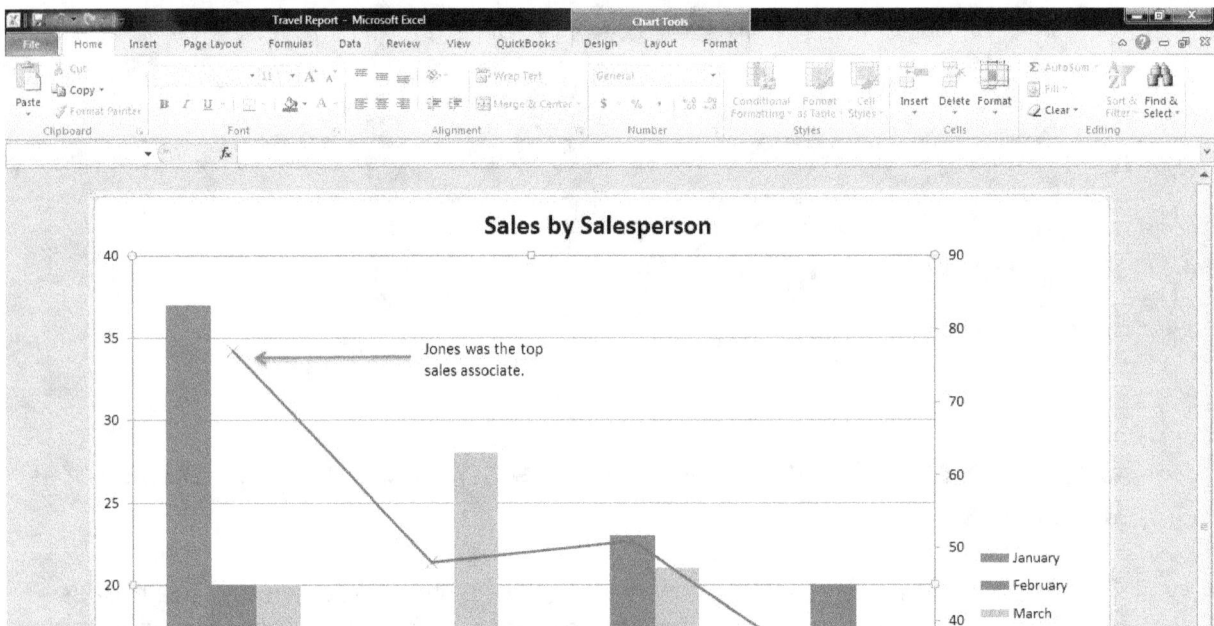

6. **Click the Textbox tool on the Layout tab. Then, draw a textbox and enter the text as shown.**

You may have to size and move the textbox to make it appear as shown.

Inserting images into charts

Excel allows you to insert picture files or clipart images into charts. You can simply insert an image such as a company logo on to the chart. Or, you can use an image of any kind as the background for the entire chart. In this portion of the lesson you will select a clipart image to be used as the background of the entire chart. You will then make adjustment to the image so it does not overpower the information on the chart.

Selecting chart elements

Up to this point you have selected different elements of the chart, such as a data series or arrow, by clicking on them. After clicking on the element you looked for sizing handles to verify you had selected that chart element. Because some elements are difficult to select by clicking on them, Excel provides an optional way to select specific elements. You can use the Chart Elements drop down list in the Format tab.

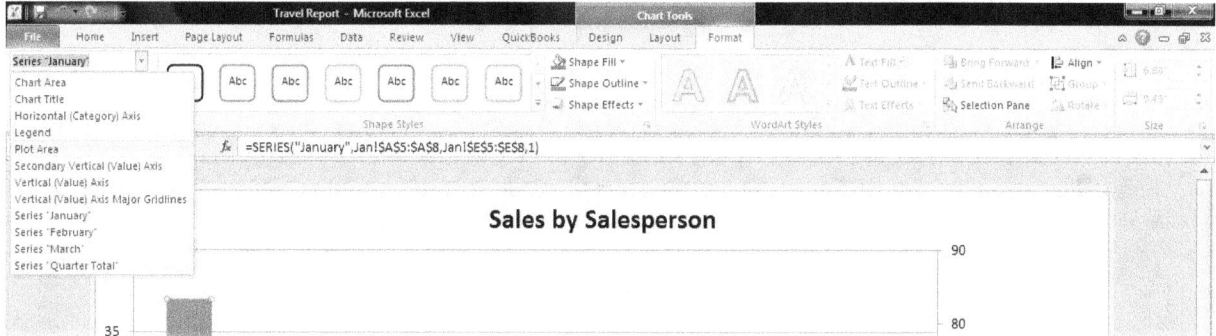

1. **Click the Chart Elements drop down list button and choose Plot Area.**

    This selects the entire plot area. You will now add a background image to the plot area of this chart.

2. **After selecting the Plot area, click the Format Selection tool just below the Chart Elements area.**

You should now see the Format Plot Area dialog box. Here you will tell Excel to use an image for the chart background.

3.   In the Format Plot area dialog box, click the Picture or texture fill radio button and then click the Clip Art… tool.

Excel will now display the clipart available on your computer. Your may not have the exact picture used in this lesson. If that is the case, pick something similar or an image of your choosing.

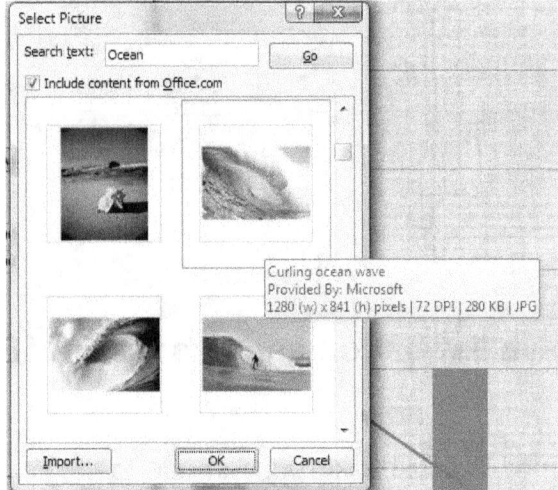

4.   In the Select Picture menu, type *Ocean* in the Search text and click Go.

Excel will now display the ocean related images in your clipart gallery.

5.   Choose the *Curling ocean wave* image and click OK.

Choose something similar if you do not have this image.

After clicking OK, Excel will return to the Format Plot Area dialog box. Here you will adjust the image's transparency so it does not overpower the chart.

6. **In the Format Plot Area, change the Transparency to 70% and click Close.**
   You should now see the adjusted clipart image as the chart's background.

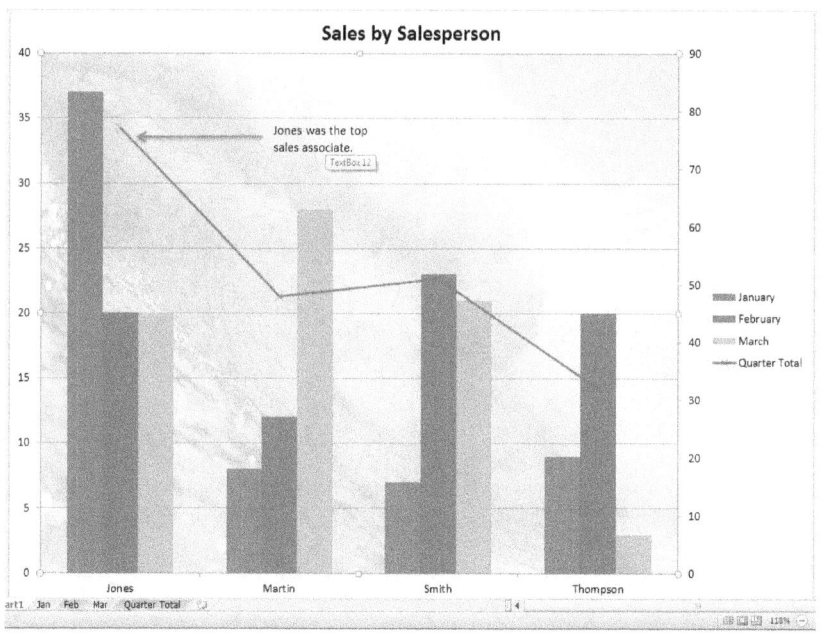

8. **Save and close the Travel Report workbook.**

Lesson #5: Some very helpful features

In this lesson you will learn to:
- *Use Group and Outline*
- *Insert Comments*
- *Use Data Validation and input messages*
- *Protect Worksheets*
- *Freeze panes*
- *Transpose data while copying*

Excel 2010: Beyond The Basics

Lesson #5: Some very helpful features

Using Auto Outline

Excel's Auto Outline feature provides a quick and easy way to summarize the data in a worksheet. This feature allows you to collapse and expand the worksheet to show the complete detail or just a summary of the worksheet. The Auto Outline recognizes formulas in your worksheet and uses them to create grouping levels. The more formula levels the worksheet has, the more flexibility you will have when using the Auto Outline feature. The Travel Report you have been working with is not very complex so the Auto Outline feature will create only two summary levels. The Auto Outline feature is available in the Data tab.

1. **Open the Travel Report workbook and select cells A4:E9 in the Jan worksheet.**

   The first step in creating an outline is to select the cells you wish to summarize.

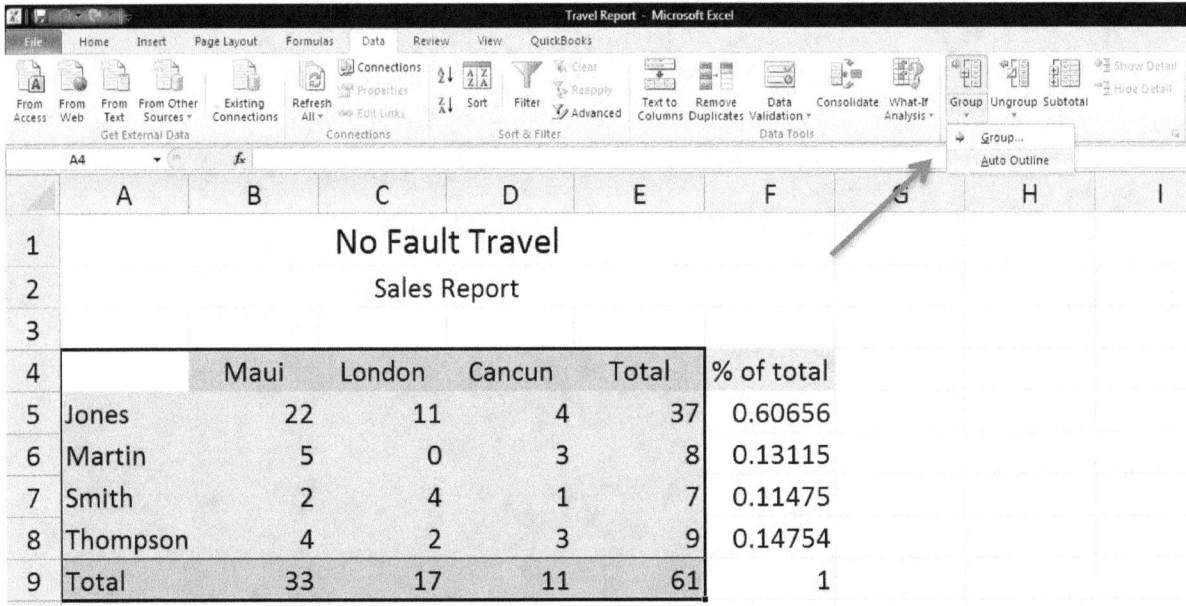

2. **In the Data tab, click the Group drop down arrow from the Outline group and select Auto Outline.**

You should now notice that Excel added some additional information above the column headings and to the left of the row headings. This tells you that Excel has created two outline levels, one vertical level and one horizontal level. As mentioned earlier, more complex worksheets may have more levels.

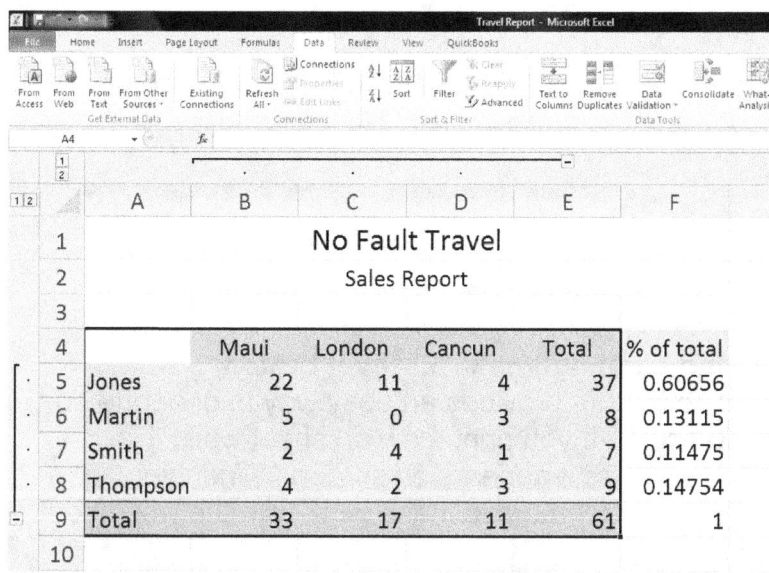

3. **Click the number 1 above and to the left of column A's heading.**
This collapses the outline in a horizontal direction. This view displays only the total for each sales associate, not the individual destinations.

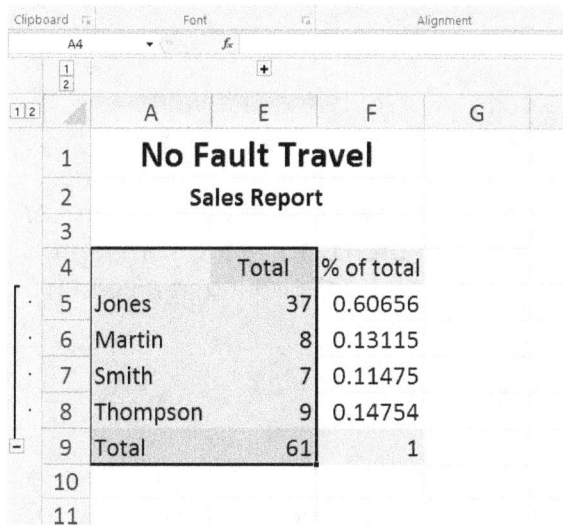

4. **Collapse the outline further by clicking the 1 above and to the left of row 1's heading.**
This collapses the outline in a vertical direction. This shows only the grand total for the month, not the individual sales associates.

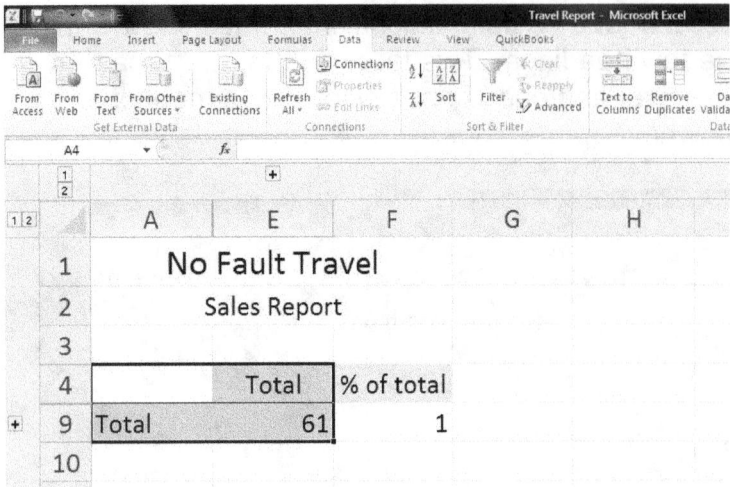

5. **Expand both views by clicking each outline's "2" level button.**

As you can see, the Auto Outline feature provides an easy way to generate an "executive summary" version of worksheets. If you print the worksheet while it is collapsed, it will appear on the printed page as it appears on screen. When you no longer have any need for the outlining, you can remove it and work with the worksheet in the normal manner.

6. **Click the drop down arrow for the Ungroup tool and choose Clear Outline.**

The outlining levels are now removed from this worksheet.

Inserting cell comments

Excel allows users to insert comments into cells. For instance, if a value in a worksheet varies greatly from the other values around it, a curious viewer of the spreadsheet may want to know why. This feature is very useful when more than one user are collaborating on a worksheet. After a comment is inserted into a cell, any user of that workbook can simply point to that cell and Excel will then display the comment associated with that cell. You can insert comments easily by right-clicking in a cell and choosing Insert Comment from the shortcut menu.

1. **Right-click on cell B5 in the Jan worksheet.**

Right-clicking provide an excellent shortcut to access many common commands and features in Excel. You can also insert comments by clicking the New Comment tool on the Review tab.

Excel 2010: Beyond The Basics

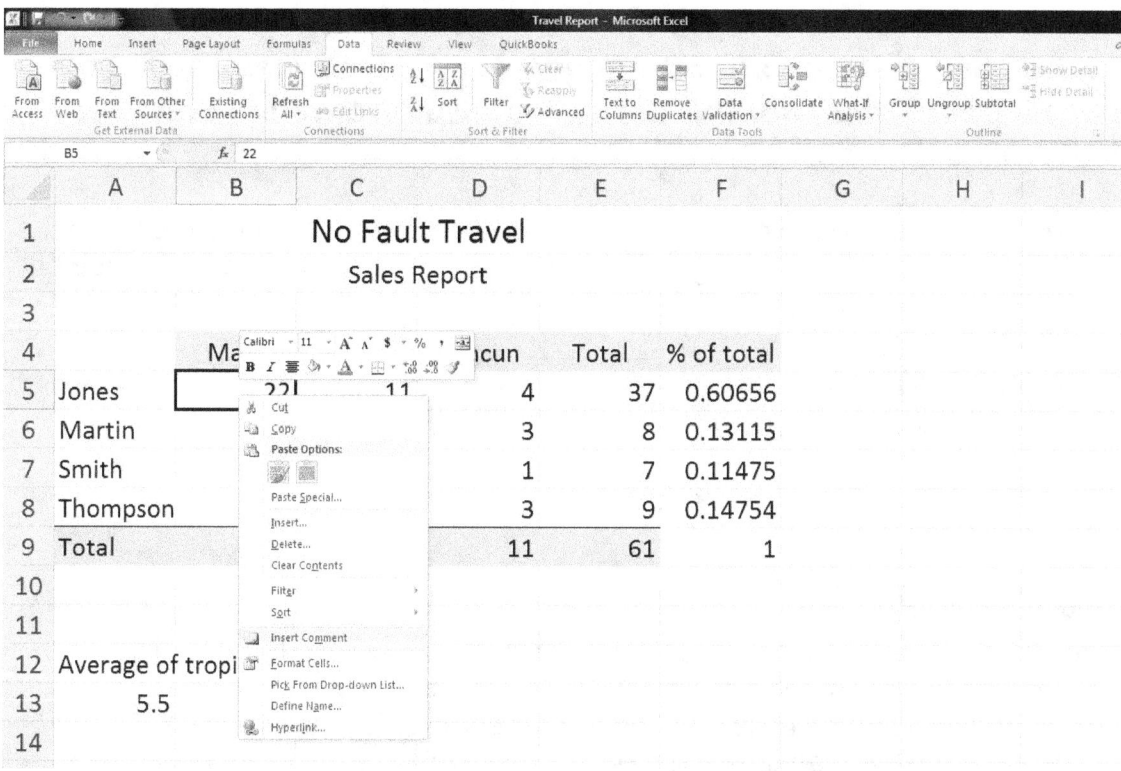

2. Choose Insert Comment from the shortcut menu.

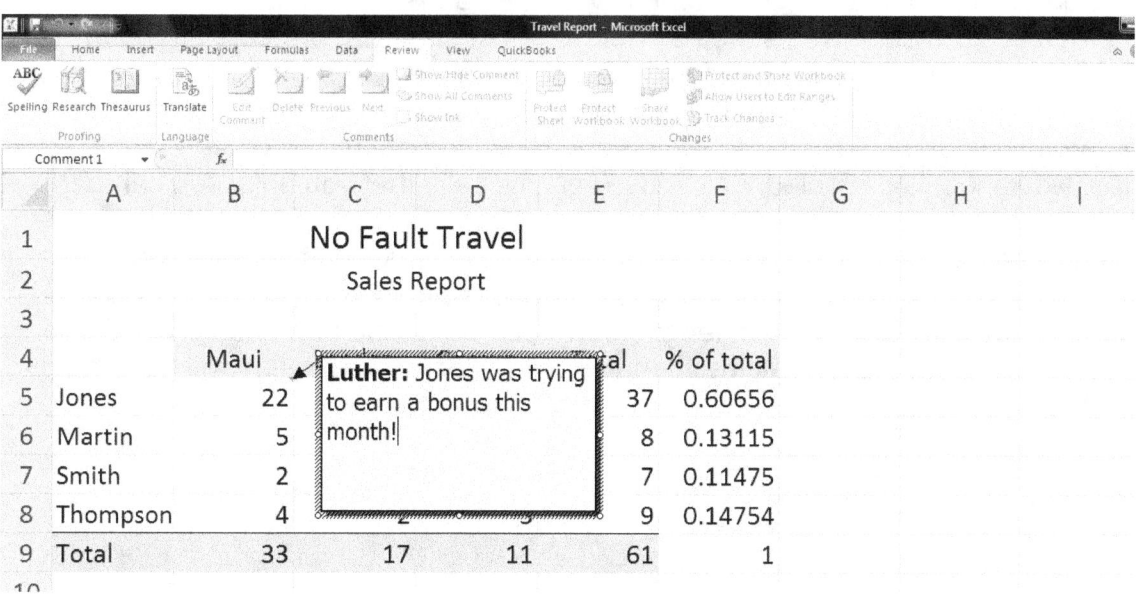

You will now see the comment text box. The comment text box also displays the name of the user. This allows several different people to insert comments in the worksheet and other users to know who inserted each comment. The name your computer displays will depend on how it was installed and your network configuration. You can change the user name from the Excel Options dialog box accessible from the Office button.

3. **In the comment box after the name, type *Jones was trying to earn a bonus this month!* then click away from the comment textbox.**

You will no longer see the entire comment. However, the cell with the comment should display a red triangle indicating that this cell has a comment. When you point at this cell the comment will expand.

4. **Point to cell B5.**
Verify that the comment expands.

5. **Save and close this workbook.**

Protecting worksheets

After spending valuable time creating the worksheet and the formulas in them you do not want to have someone accidentally erase formulas that took you hours to create. You can easily prevent this by protecting specific cells in a worksheet. Protected cells cannot be changed or erased. To use worksheets you want to have some cells that can be changed and others, such as cells that contain formulas, protected. Like the ability to insert comments, cell protection is a feature that is very useful when multiple users are collaborating with the same workbook.

When you protect a worksheet, by default, all cells will be protected. This would mean that no cells in the worksheet could ever be changed. This would not make a very useful worksheet. If you want users to be able to change certain cells, you must turn the protection off in those cells before you protect the entire worksheet. Then, once the entire worksheet is protected, only those specific cells that you unlocked can be changed.

In this portion of this lesson you will protect the formulas in the Loan Amortization workbook you created earlier. You will unlock the cells that need to change for each loan, such as the interest rate, loan length, down payment, and purchase price. The rest of the workbook, including all the formulas will be locked and users will be unable to change them.

1. **Open the Loan Amortization workbook.**

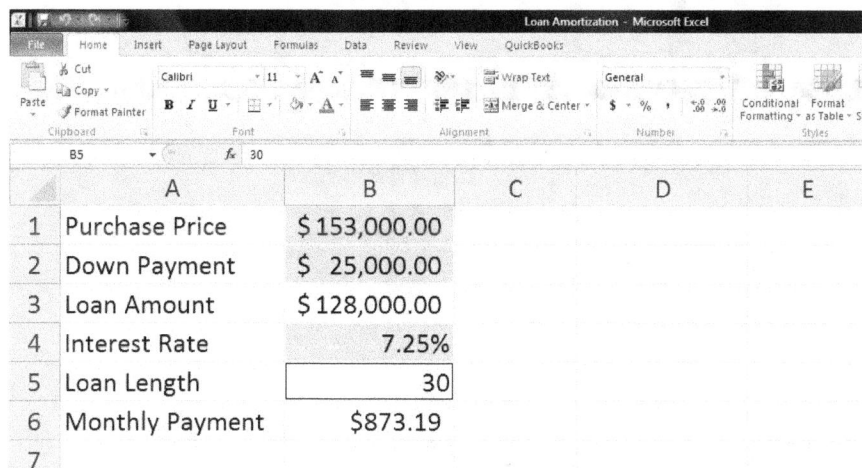

2. **Use the (Control) key to select cells B1, B2, B4, and B5.**
These are the only cells that users need to change in this worksheet as you enter additional loan information. Worksheet protection can be turned off should you ever need to change formulas or create new ones in the worksheet. Remember that the (Control) key allows you to select non-contiguous cells or ranges.

3. **Carefully right-click in the selected cells and choose Format Cells to launch the Format Cells dialog box.**

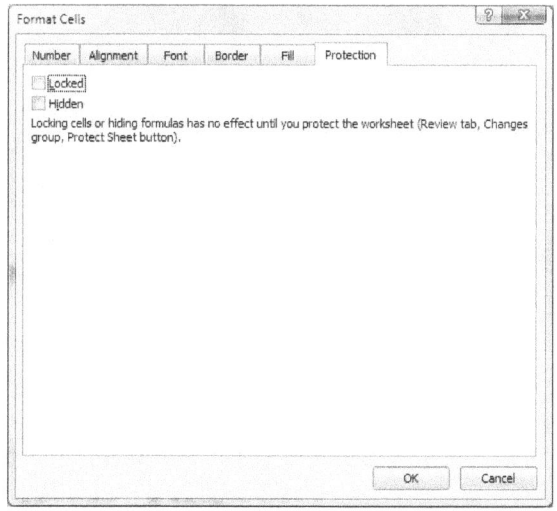

You could also display this dialog box by clicking the dialog box launcher on the ribbon from either the Font or Alignment groups on the Home tab.

4. **In the Format Cells dialog box, click the Protection tab and turn off the Locked option and click OK.**

This tells Excel not to lock these cells when you enable worksheet protection. Protection is a two-step process. First you unlock the cells you do not want protected and then protect the entire worksheet.

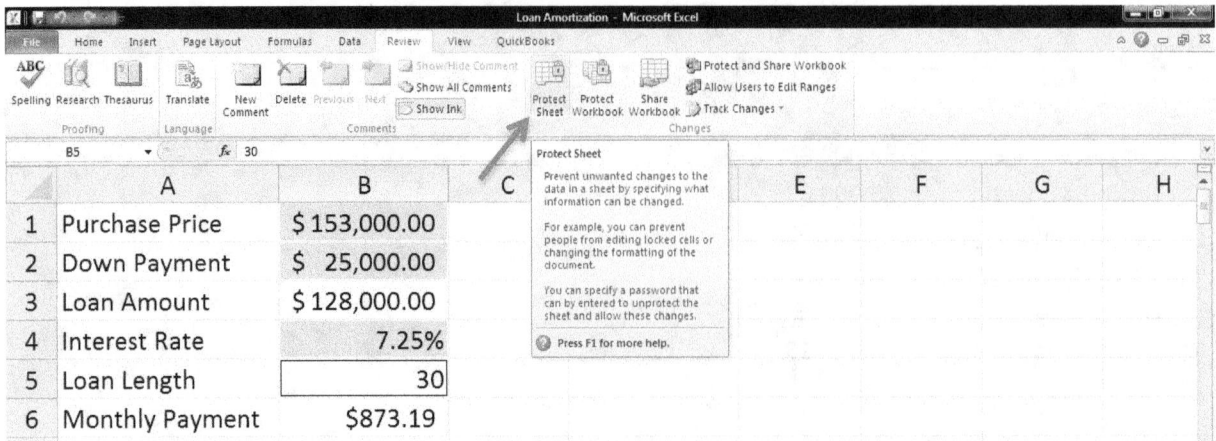

5. **Click the Protect Sheet tool in the Review tab.**

   You should now see the Protect Sheet dialog box. This dialog box allows you to specify how much users can do with the worksheet when it is protected. It also gives you the option of adding a password that would be required to un-protect the worksheet. Use passwords sparingly, especially with company owned data. If you do need password protection, make sure someone else in your company knows your passwords. You do not want to leave your company hanging with a workbook they cannot alter after you no longer work for that company.

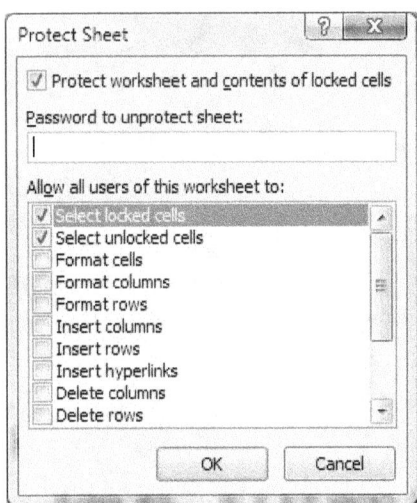

6. **Click OK with the default options in the Protect Sheet dialog box.**
   You are not adding a password for this lesson.

   Now you will try to alter a protected cell.

7. Move to cell D9 and press (Delete).

You should see a message informing you that this is a protected cell.

8. Click OK in the warning message.
You can alter unlocked cells but not cells that are protected after turning on Worksheet protection.

Using Data Validation and Input Messages

Data Validation allows you to specify the range of values and type of information that can be entered into unlocked cells. For example, in the loan amortization worksheet, assume that the interest rate must be between 1% and 10%. Creating a validation rule for the interest rate cell would prevent improper data from being entered into that cell.

In addition to Data Validation, Excel also allows you to create instructions that appear when you move into a particular cell. These are called Input Messages.

In this lesson you will add Data Validation rules and Input Messages to cells in the Loan Amortization worksheet. You can access this feature from the Data group. However, to add Data Validation rules, the worksheet must be unprotected.

1. From the Review tab, Changes group, choose Unprotect Sheet.

The sheet is now unprotected. You will protect it again after making these changes. Unprotecting a worksheet that is not password protected can be done by any user. However, if the user is savvy enough to know how to unprotect a worksheet, he or she is also probably savvy enough not to destroy your formulas. But, just in case, it is a good idea to keep a master copy of the workbook before distributing it to other users.

2. Move to cell B4 and choose Data Validation in the Data Tools group from the Data tab.

Excel 2010: Beyond The Basics

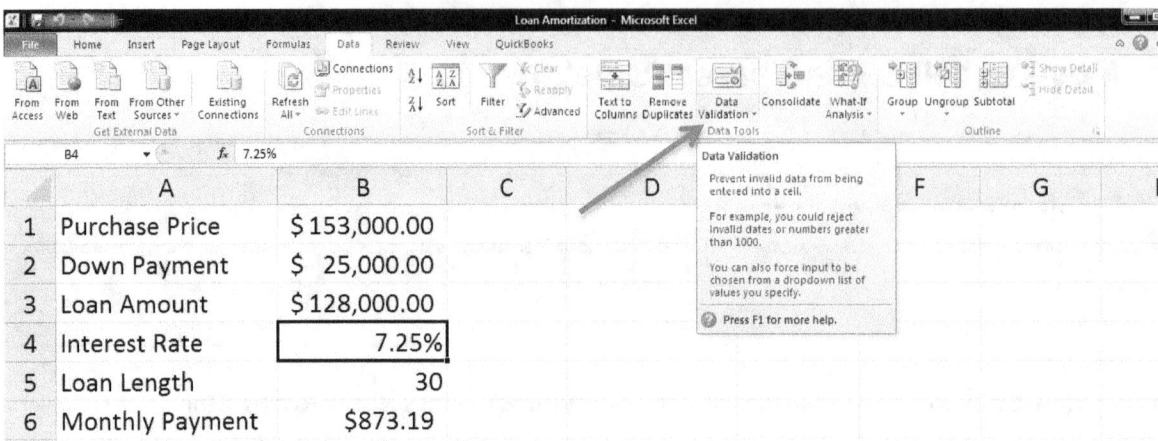

You should now see the Data Validation dialog box. Here you can specify rules for the values that you will allow to be entered into this cell. For this lesson we will allow a range of interest rates.

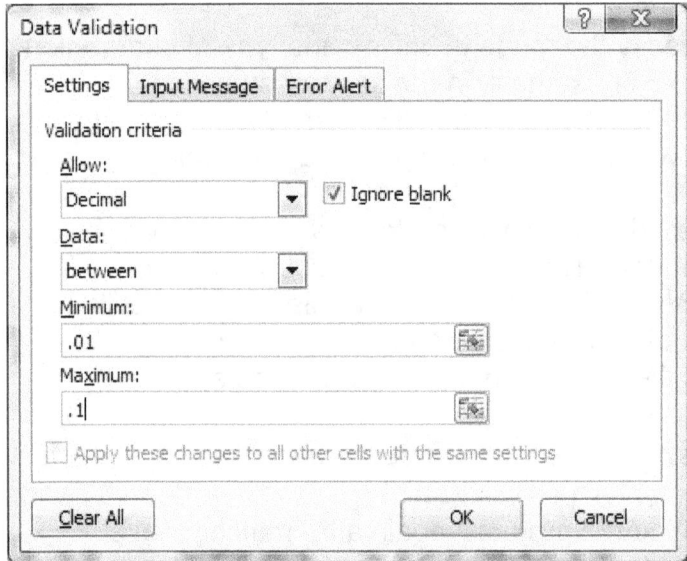

3. **In the Settings tab, change the Allow setting to Decimal.**
You have now told Excel that you will allow decimal values in this cell, instead of whole numbers, dates, or any value at all.

4. **Select *between* in the Data drop-down list.**
You are allowing users to enter a range of values. You could choose other operators here such as *less than* or *greater than*.

5. **Enter *.01* in the Minimum and *.1* in the Maximum settings.**
The Validation rule ensures that only these values will be processed in the loan amortization. Remember that mathematically 1% is entered into Excel as .01. So with this rule, you are allowing only values between 1% and 10% in this cell.

Now you will add an input message that will guide users working with this workbook. The input message will let them know the values that are valid for this cell.

6. Click the Input Message tab in the Data Validation dialog box.

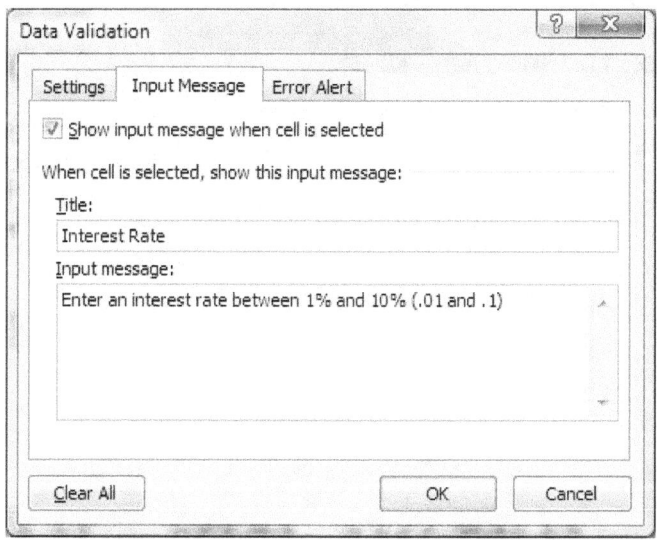

7. Type *Interest Rate* in the Title and then type *Enter an interest rate between 1% and 10% (.01 and .1)* in the Input message section.

This message will be displayed when users enter cell B4.

Now you will add an error message that will display when users violate the validation rule you just established.

8. Click the Error Alert tab and enter the information shown in the Title and Error message text areas.

The Error Alert text will be displayed if an incorrect interest rate is entered into cell B4.

9. **Click OK after entering this information in the Data Validation dialog box.**

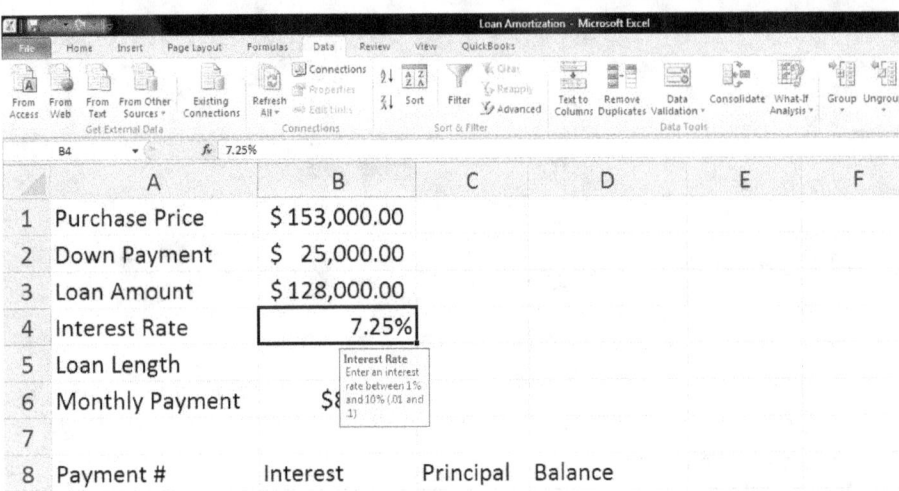

10. **Move to cell B4 and verify the Input Message is displayed.**
    This message appears similar to the comment you inserted earlier.

11. **In cell B4 type *.15* and press (Enter).**
    You should see an error message informing you that this is not a correct value.

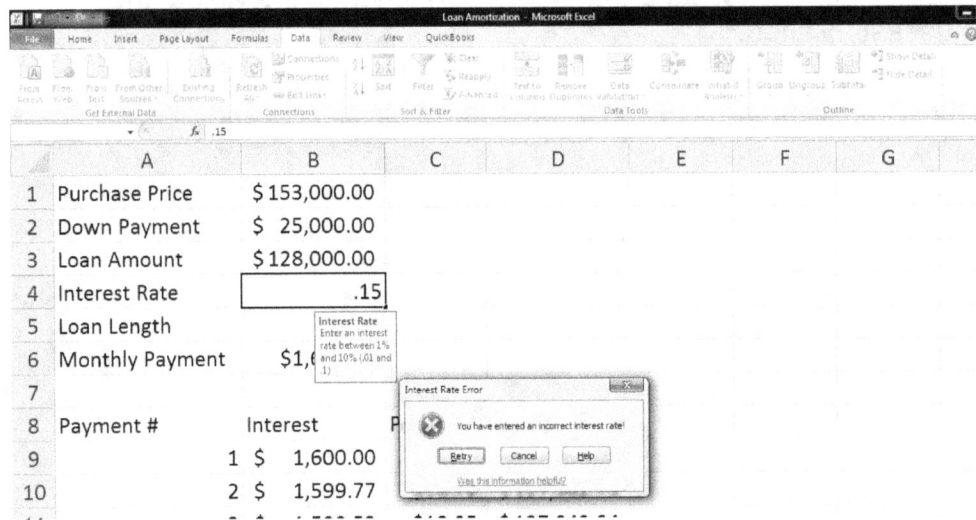

12. **Press (Escape) or click Cancel to return to the original interest rate.**

Freezing worksheet panes

In large worksheets you may often need to scroll vertically or horizontally so far that you can no longer see information like column or row headings that help you identify the information in your worksheet. For example, assume you are using a worksheet with column headings for the months of January through June. As you enter several rows of information for each month you may scroll down and no longer be able to see the column headings. In this case, you could get confused and possibly enter data in the wrong column.

You can solve this problem by freezing worksheet panes. When you freeze panes in your worksheet, you can scroll around the worksheet and always see column or row headings.

Freezing always takes place above and to the left of the current cells. So, to freeze worksheet panes, move below and to the right of the rows and columns you want frozen. You can find the Freeze Panes command in the View tab. In this portion of the lesson you will freeze the panes in the loan amortization schedule.

1.   Move to cell A9 in Sheet1 of the loan amortization workbook.

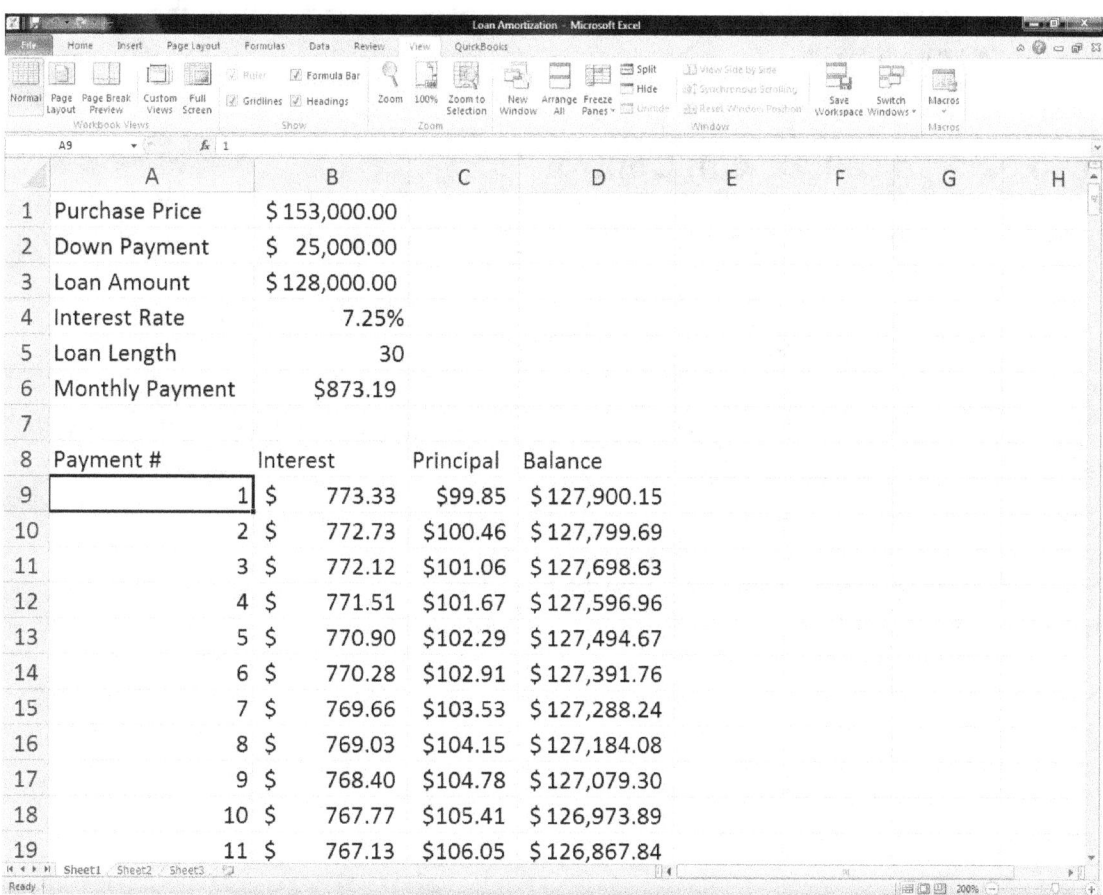

Because Excel freezes above and to the left, when you freeze the panes in this worksheet, the first 8 rows will always be displayed, even when you scroll down several hundred rows.

2. **Switch to the View tab and click the Freeze Panes tool in the Window group.**

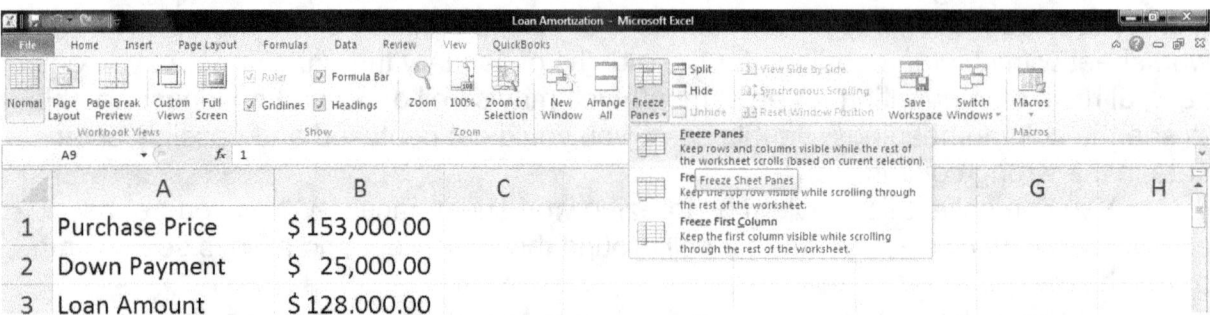

3. **Choose Freeze Panes, the top option from the list of choices.**
   This will freeze all rows above cell A9 and all columns to the left, which in this case there are none.

4. **Press (page down) several times to scroll down the worksheet.**
   As you do, you should always be able to see the loan information in the first seven rows of the worksheet.

5. **Move back to cell A9 with Control+Home.**
   When no panes are frozen, Control+Home takes you to cell A1. When panes are frozen, this command takes you to the top of the current pane, in this case, cell A9.

   You will now unfreeze the panes and scroll down again so you can clearly see the difference freezing panes makes in a worksheet.

6. **Click the Freeze Panes tool again and this time select Unfreeze Panes from the available options.**

7. **Press (page down) several times again.**
   This time you should notice that the first several rows are not frozen.

Using the copy command to transpose data

Transposing means to switch the orientation of data. When you transpose data, the column headings will become the row headings and vise-versa. In this portion of the exercise you will copy and transpose as you paste. To accomplish this you will use the Paste Special command.

1. In the Loan Amortization workbook, select cells A1 through B6 then click the Copy command on the Home tab.

This is just one of the ways you can select the Copy command. When Excel provides several ways to select the same command, there is no one right way to do it. The right way is the way you prefer and remember.

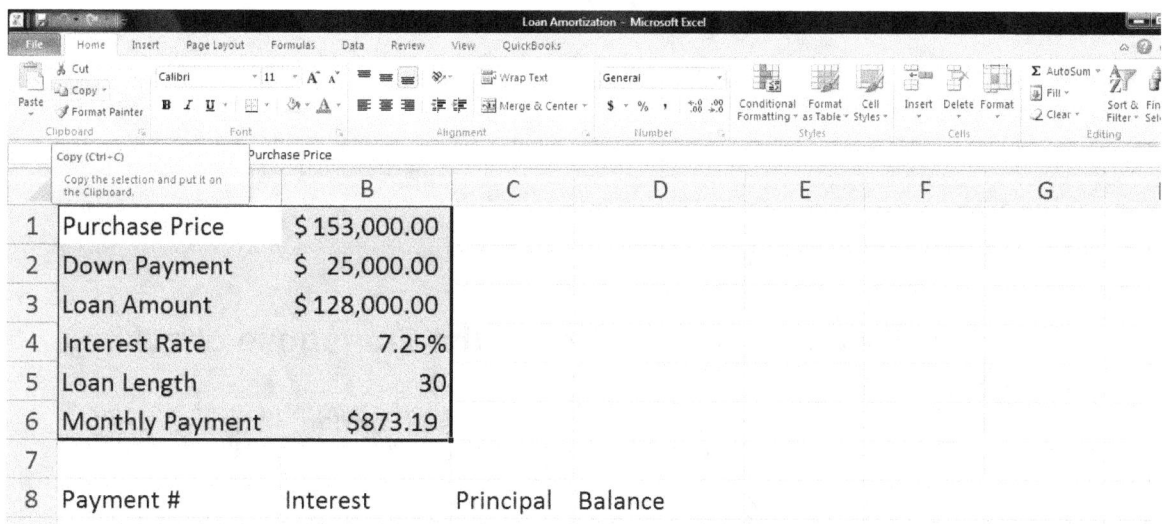

2. Select Sheet2 and ensure cell A1 is active in this sheet.
You will place the copy of the cells you have selected on this sheet.

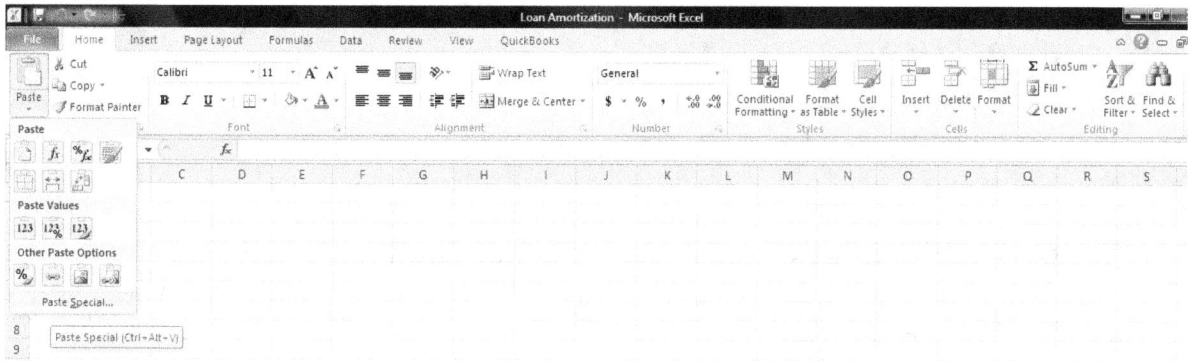

3. Click the drop down arrow on the Paste tool and choose Paste Special.

The paste special command gives you access to many useful methods of pasting. You can, for example, copy the values that result from formulas instead of the formulas themselves. Or, you can use the Paste Special command to copy only the formatting in the selected cells. Or, as in this case, you can use it to transpose the data.

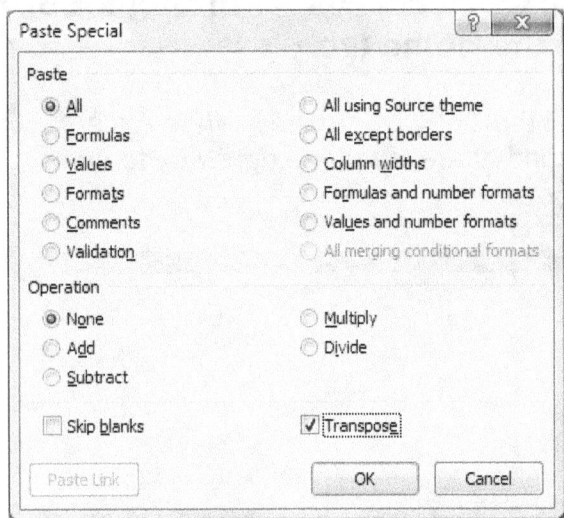

4. **In the Paste Special dialog box, click the Transpose checkbox and click OK.**

You should now see the copied data in a transposed format. Increase the column widths on Sheet2 so the numbers will display properly.

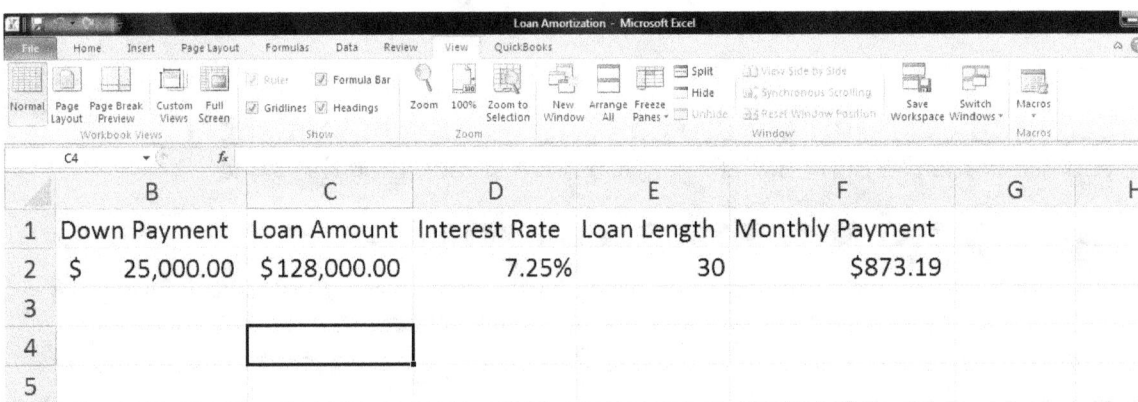

5. **Move back to Sheet1 and then protect the worksheet again.**

You unprotected the worksheet to add the Data Validation rules and experiment with freezing worksheet panes.

6. **Save and close the worksheet.**

Lesson #6: Excel Templates

In this lesson you will learn to:
- *Create Excel Templates*
- *Use Excel Templates*

Lesson #6: Excel Templates

When you open a new workbook it is blank. You have to enter all the data, formulas and formatting you need to use it. If you are working in a situation where you are using the same type of workbook over and over again, creating it every time from scratch makes no sense. You have probably already realized that and if you are reusing the same type of workbook you have probably created a master version of the file. Then, when you need that worksheet you probably just open up the master and enter the pertinent data.

Using a master version of a workbook is certainly better than recreating it every time. However, there is always a danger, even if it is slight, of forgetting to save the file with a new name after entering data and writing over the master copy. This is certainly not a fatal error, but it takes time the next time to erase the data you should not have saved in the master. Also, it takes a little time to find the master file using the open command because it is probably stored in a large list of Excel workbooks you are currently using.

Excel templates are an optional feature that can make reusing a workbook faster and easier. Instead of opening an existing workbook, when using a template you use the New command. Then, after entering the data you need, if you accidentally choose Save rather than Save As, there is no danger of writing over the template because Excel forces you to give your New template-based workbook a name. The template is protected from being overwritten unless you purposely do so.

In this lesson you will use a predefined Excel template. You will also create your own template based on the Amortization Schedule. In this lesson you will also learn some more about Excel formulas, specifically the IF() function.

Using predefined templates

Excel comes with many predefined templates for you to use. To use one of Excel's templates, you will choose the New command from the File menu. But, instead of choosing Blank Workbook, you will choose a predefined template. In this portion of the lesson you will use a Packing List template from Office.com.

1. **Close any open Workbooks and open the File menu and choose New.**

Notice that in addition to the Blank workbook template, Excel has many other templates available for your use.

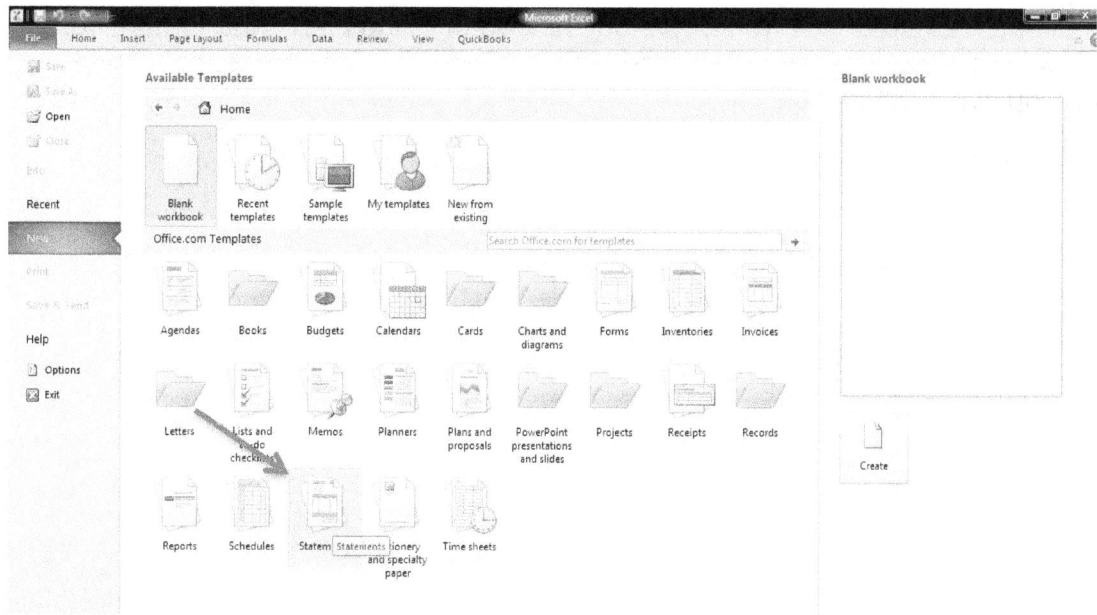

2. In the list of Office.com templates, click Statements.
Excel will now display several templates available in this category.

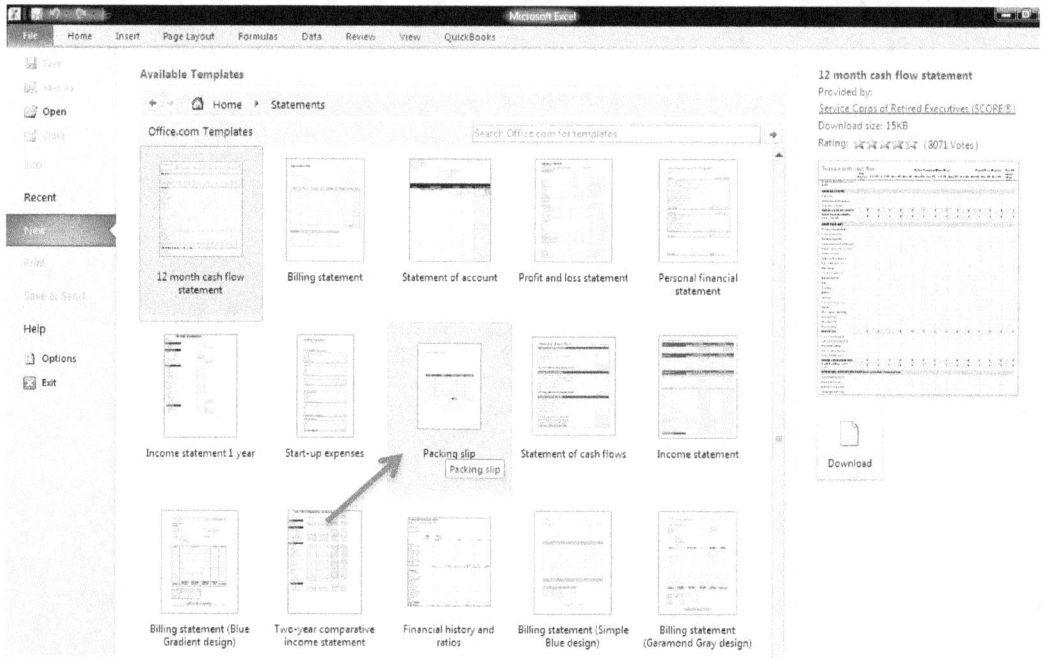

3. In the list of templates, double-click Packing slip.

You can also click on it once and click the Download tool at the right of the screen. It is also possible that your organization does not let you download templates, even from Office.com. If this is the case, skip this part the lesson and move to the Creating a template section.

Excel has created a new workbook, but instead of being blank, the formatting and formulas for this packing slip are already there. The next step is to simply enter the information you want and save it.

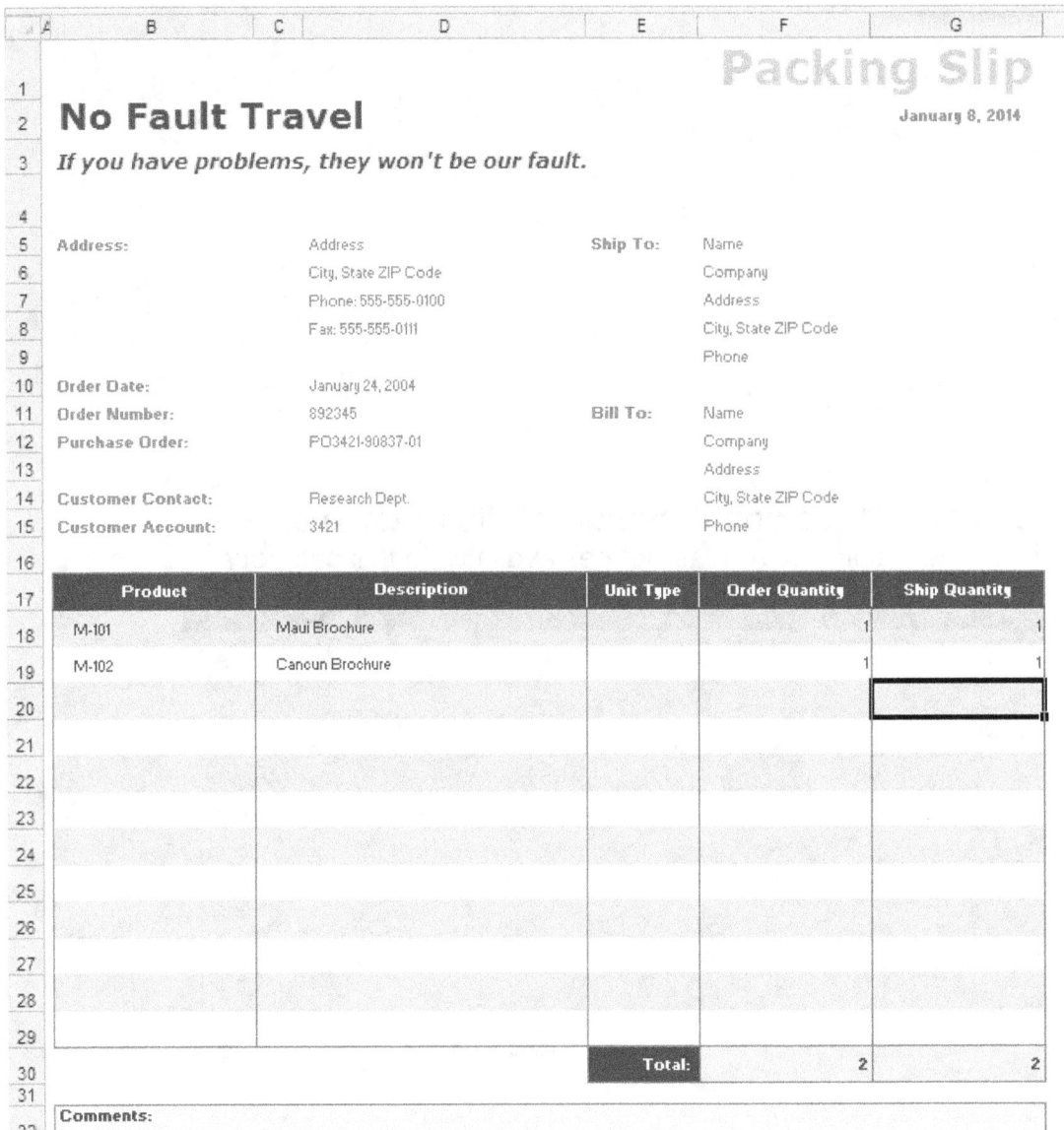

4. **Enter information similar to that shown and choose the Save command, not Save As.**

When you choose the Save command, Excel still asks you to name the file. This is because you created this using a template rather than opening and reusing an existing workbook.

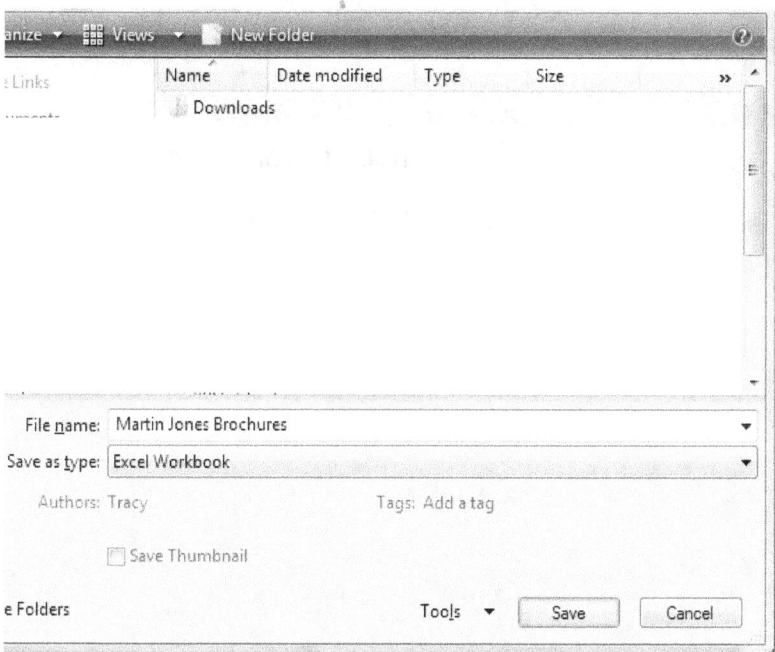

5. Enter a file name of *Martin Jones Brochure* and click Save. Close all open workbooks.

Excel has numerous templates for you to use. There is even a template for a loan amortization, but using that one would take away all the fun of the next part of this lesson. If Excel's predefined templates do not meet your needs perfectly you can even modify and save them as your own templates. In the next part of this lesson you will learn how to save a workbook as a template.

Creating your own template

To create your own Excel templates the first step is to create master version of the workbook. Just as the packing slip you just used, your own templates should have all the formatting and formulas already created. The only thing your template will not have is the actual data used in creating a new version of the workbook based on the template.

To create a template you will open the Loan Amortization workbook you created earlier. Before turning it into a template you will make several modifications to the formulas and formatting already in this workbook.

1. Open the Loan Amortization workbook and turn off protection.

You can find the Unprotect sheet tool in the Review tab. You are turning off worksheet protection because you will be making many modifications before turning this into an Excel template.

2. **Change the loan length to 1 year instead of 30.**

3. **Increase the width of the Column C to view all values.**
   Double-clicking on the edge of a column quickly changes to column width.

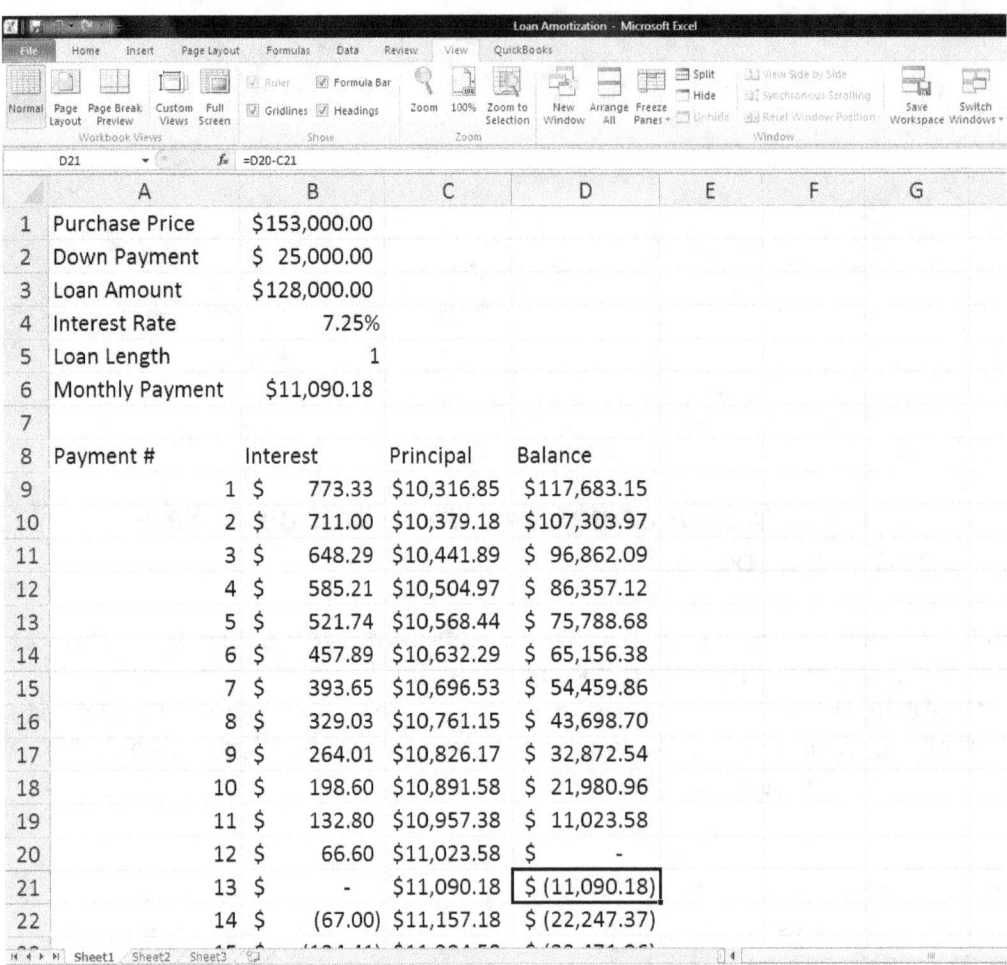

When you originally created this workbook, you created formulas for 30 years of payments. Now, as you changed the length of the loan to only one year, you can see this causes the worksheet to begin computing a negative balance after the loan is paid off. You will now modify the formulas in the amortization schedule so they do not compute values after the loan has been paid off. You will do this by using the IF() function.

Excel 2010: Beyond The Basics

[Screenshot of Excel spreadsheet showing a Loan Amortization worksheet. Key values visible:]

	A	B	C	D
1	Purchase Price	$153,000.00		
2	Down Payment	$ 25,000.00		
3	Loan Amount	$128,000.00		
4	Interest Rate	7.25%		
5	Loan Length	1		
6	Monthly Payment	$11,090.18		
7				
8	Payment #	Interest	Principal	Balance
9	1	$ 773.33	$10,316.85	$117,683.15
10	=IF(B9="","",IF((A9+1)>($B$5*12),"",A9+1))			$107,303.97
11		648.29	$10,441.89	$ 96,862.09
12	4	$ 585.21	$10,504.97	$ 86,357.12
13	5	$ 521.74	$10,568.44	$ 75,788.68
14	6	$ 457.89	$10,632.29	$ 65,156.38
15	7	$ 393.65	$10,696.53	$ 54,459.86
16	8	$ 329.03	$10,761.15	$ 43,698.70
17	9	$ 264.01	$10,826.17	$ 32,872.54
18	10	$ 198.60	$10,891.58	$ 21,980.96
19	11	$ 132.80	$10,957.38	$ 11,023.58
20	12	$ 66.60	$11,023.58	$ -
21	13	$ -	$11,090.18	$ (11,090.18)
22	14	$ (67.00)	$11,157.18	$ (22,247.37)

4. **Move to cell A10 and enter the formula**
   =IF(B9="","",IF((A9+1)>($B$5*12),"",A9+1))

   This formula uses nested IF() functions because there are two conditions it will examine. This formula tells Excel to first check the payment number above. If the cell for the payment number is blank (""), then make that cell blank. In other words, if the loan is paid off, the payment numbers do not need to increment all the way to 360 as it does now.

   Then, if the payment number in the cell above this one is NOT empty, this formula has Excel check to see if this payment number should be empty because the loan is paid off with the pervious payment. It does this by comparing the payment number that should be in this cell, the cell above it plus one (A9+1), to the number of payments in the entire loan (B5*12). Because you will be copying this to many other cells, the absolute reference is necessary because you will compare every payment number to the length of the loan in cell B5. Finally, if this is a valid payment number, it adds 1 to the payment number above it (A9+1).

5. **Press (Enter) after typing the formula.**

Excel 2010: Beyond The Basics

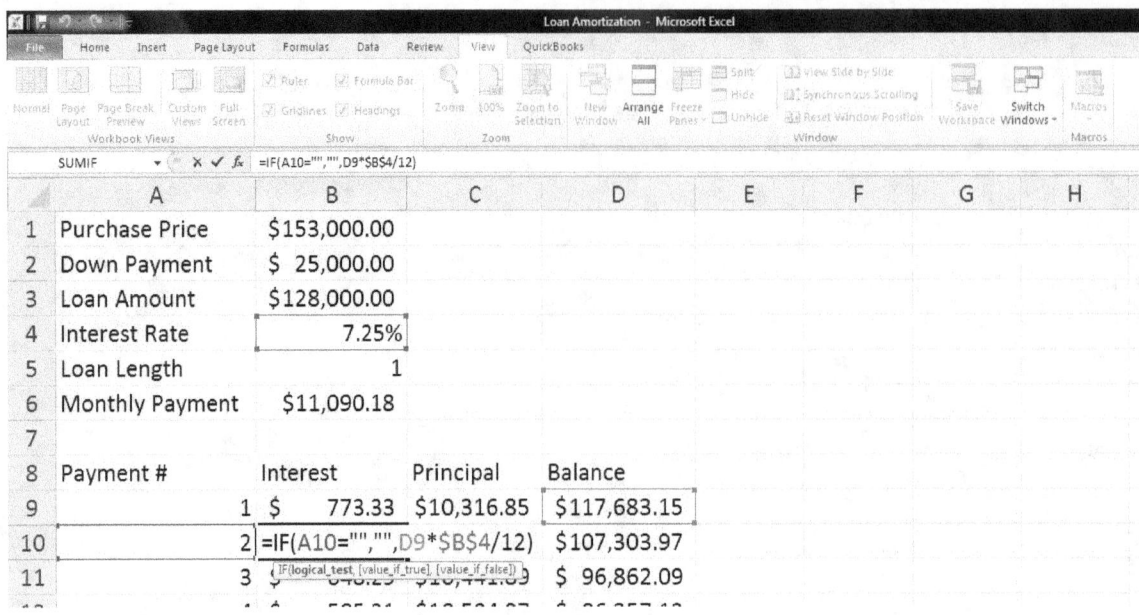

6. **Move to cell B10, the interest for the second payment, and enter the following formula: =IF(A10="","",D9*$B$4/12).**
   This formula checks to see if this is a valid payment by checking to see if the payment number cell is blank (=""). If the payment number cell is not blank, it then computes the interest for that payment. This cell still computes the same formula it did before, but now only when the payment number cell is not blank.

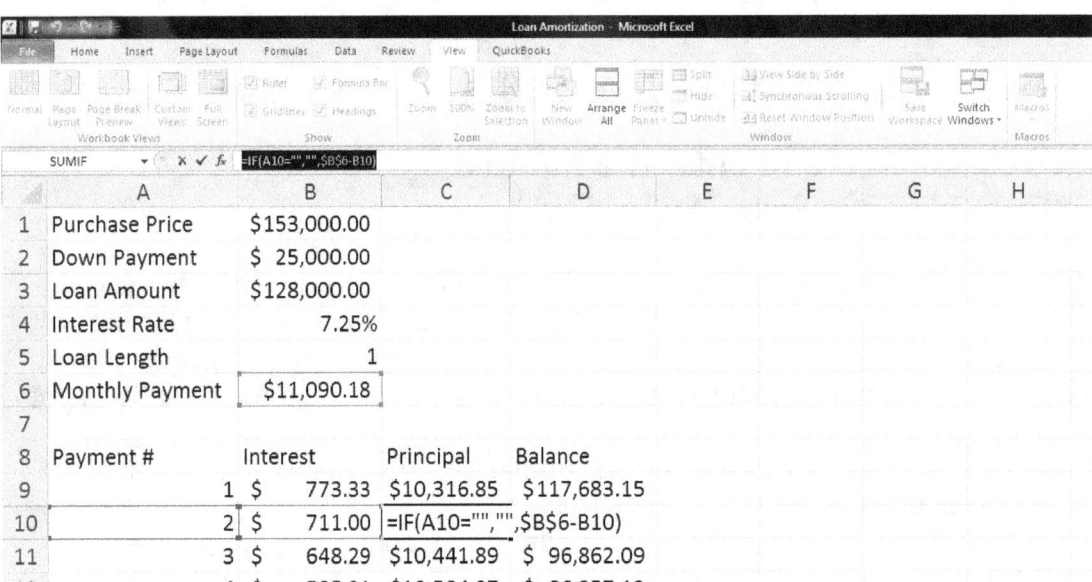

7. **Move to cell C10, the principal for the second payment, and enter the following formula: =IF(A10="","",$B$6-B10).**
   Like this interest computation, this formula only computes the principal for the loan if this is a valid payment.

Excel 2010: Beyond The Basics

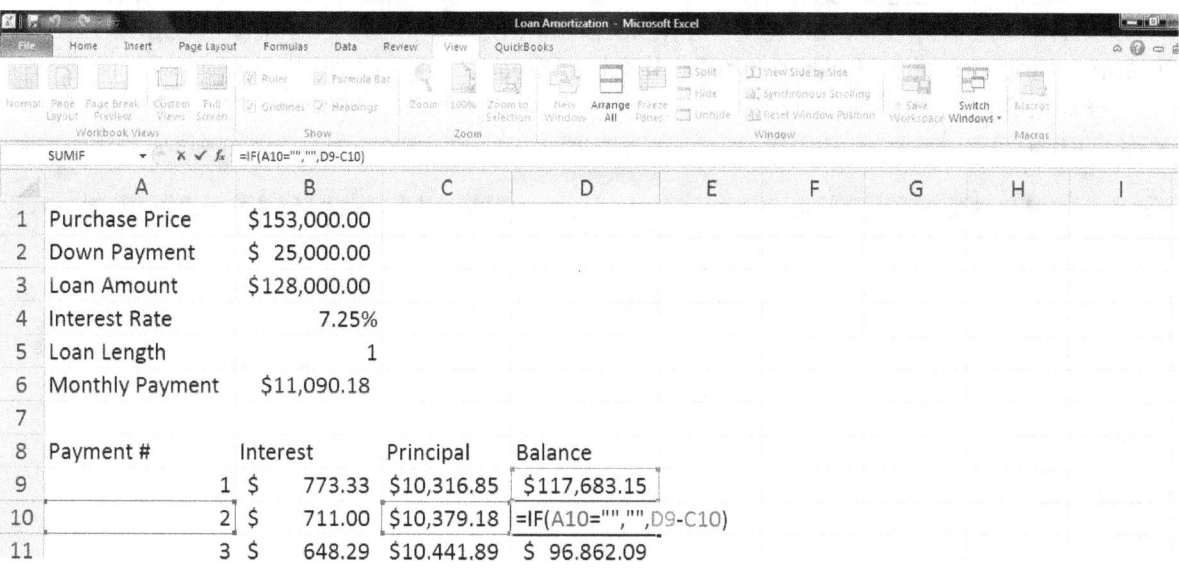

8. **Move to cell D10, the Balance for the second payment. and enter the following formula: =IF(A10="","",D9-C10).**

Like the other formulas, this one checks to see if the payment number is empty. If this payment number cell is not empty, it computes the balance after this payment is made.

Now you will copy these new formulas into all the cells that currently contain formulas for the loan amortization schedule.

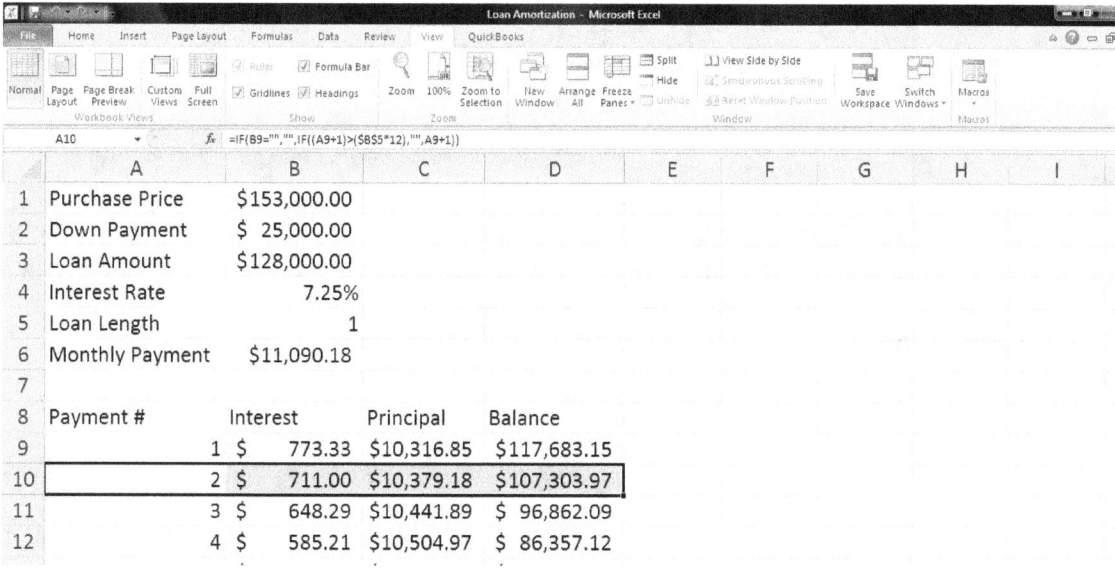

9. **Select cells A10 through D10. Then, double-click the fill handle to copy these formulas.**

After copying these cells you should notice the formulas stop computing after one year of payments. By adding the If() function to these formulas you have stopped Excel from computing negative balances after the loan is paid off. Even though this worksheet stops computing after 12 payments, there are still formulas down to row 368, so you can enter a loan length of up to 30 years and still have an amortization schedule.

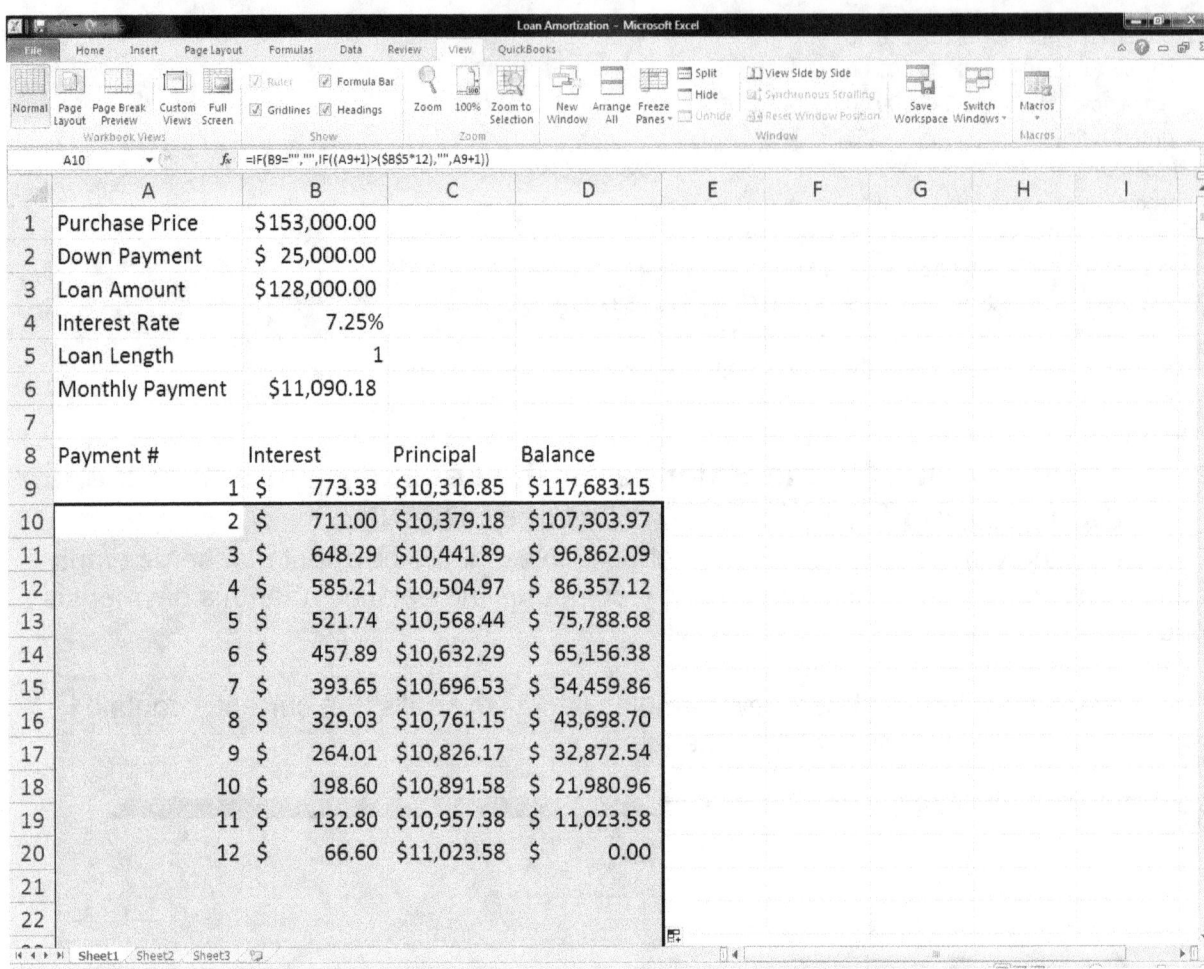

You are almost ready to turn this workbook into a template. However, before you do that you will add a few other features to make this even more user friendly. This will include adding input messages to the Purchase Price, Down Payment, and Loan Length cells. You will also add some shading to these cells to enhance the appearance of the template.

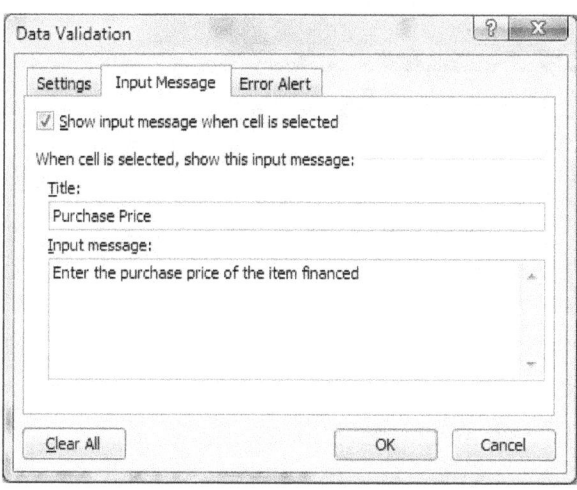

10. Move to cell B1 and enter the input message as shown.
You can find the Data Validation tool in the Data tab.

11. In cell B2 enter the input message: *Enter the down payment made on this purchase.*

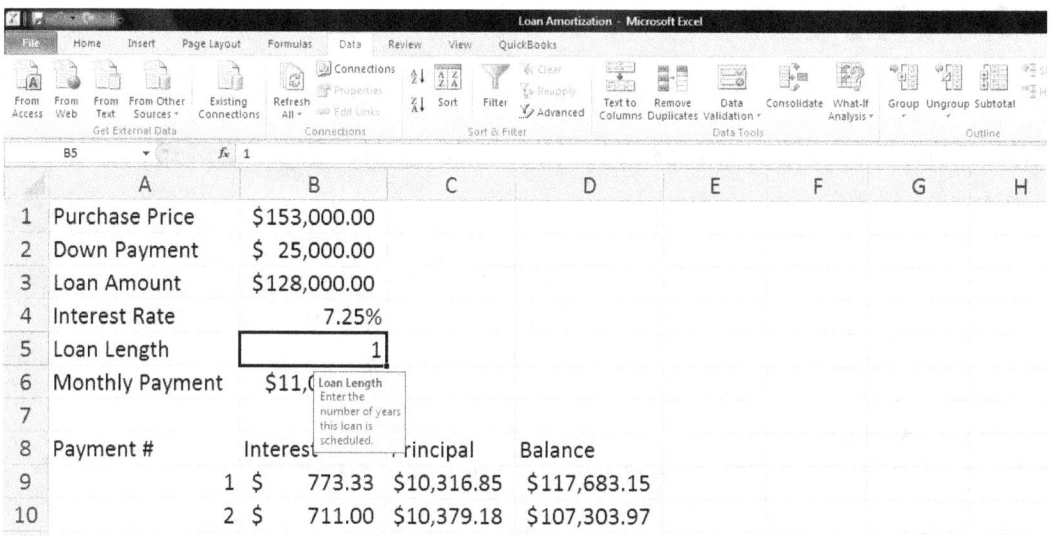

12. In cell B5 enter the input message: *Enter the number of years this loan is scheduled.*

You already added an input message to the interest rate in an earlier lesson.

	A	B	C	D	E
1	Purchase Price	$153,000.00			
2	Down Payment	$ 25,000.00			
3	Loan Amount	$128,000.00			
4	Interest Rate	7.25%			
5	Loan Length	1			
6	Monthly Payment	$11,090.18			
7					
8	Payment #	Interest		Principal	Balance
9	1	$	773.33	$10,316.85	$117,683.15
10	2	$	711.00	$10,379.18	$107,303.97
11	3	$	648.29	$10,441.89	$ 96,862.09
12	4	$	585.21	$10,504.97	$ 86,357.12
13	5	$	521.74	$10,568.44	$ 75,788.68
14	6	$	457.89	$10,632.29	$ 65,156.38
15	7	$	393.65	$10,696.53	$ 54,459.86
16	8	$	329.03	$10,761.15	$ 43,698.70
17	9	$	264.01	$10,826.17	$ 32,872.54
18	10	$	198.60	$10,891.58	$ 21,980.96
19	11	$	132.80	$10,957.38	$ 11,023.58
20	12	$	66.60	$11,023.58	$ 0.00

13. Add shading and outside cell borders to cells B1, B2, B4, and B5.

You are almost ready to turn this workbook into a template. Before you do that you will turn Worksheet protection back on and delete the values used in the loan payment computation.

14. Protect the worksheet.
This tool is in the Review tab. Leave the default options selected.

15. Delete the values in cells B1, B2, B4, and B5.
You will see some errors in the first payment row. You could correct this by adding IF statements to these formulas too, but since all loans will have at least one payment, this payment row will not display errors as soon as data is entered into the cells you just deleted.

Saving a workbook as a template

You are now ready to turn this workbook into an Excel template. To do this you will use the Save As command. In addition to entering a name for this template, you will also change the file type from Excel workbook to Excel template.

1. Open the File menu and choose the Save As command.

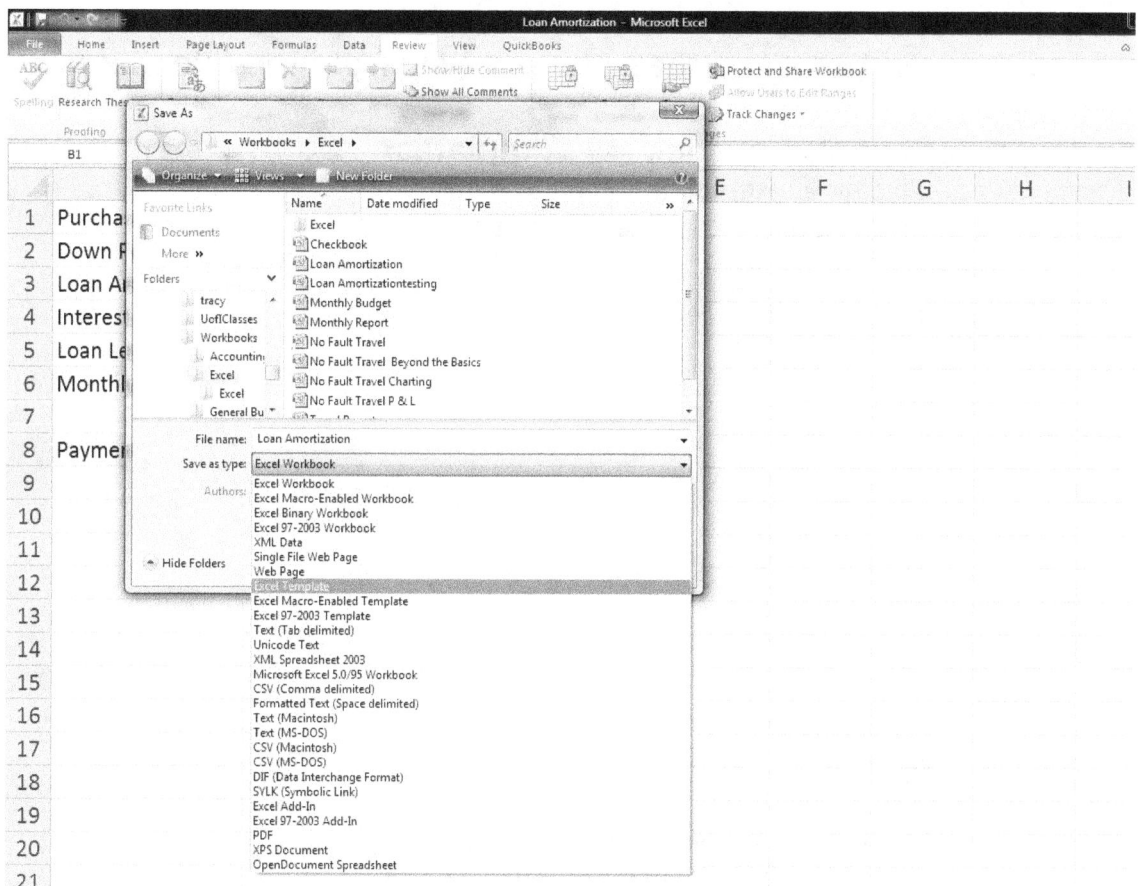

2. In the Save As dialog box, leave the file name as is but click the Save as type drop down list and choose Excel Template, then click Save.

Your workbook has now been saved as a template. Next, you will create a new workbook based on the template you just created.

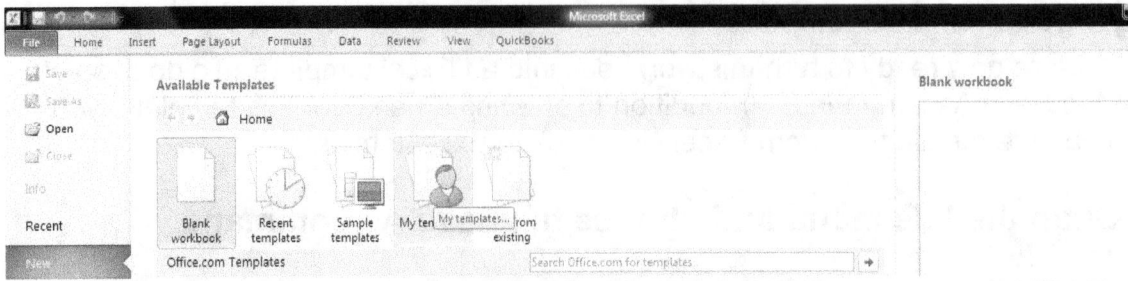

3. **Close the workbook and then choose New from the File menu.**

4. **In the list of templates, click My Templates.**
    Excel will now display any templates you have downloaded or created. Among these will be the Loan Amortization template you just created.

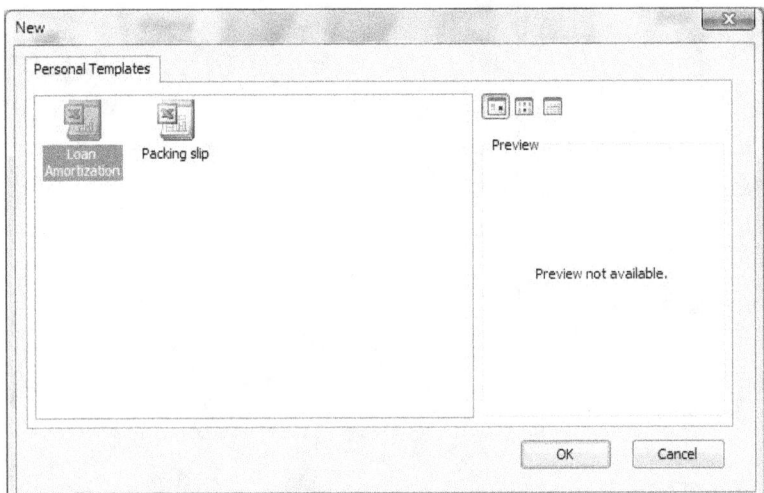

5. **Select the Loan Amortization template and click OK.**

    Excel will now create a new workbook based on the Loan Amortization template.

Excel 2010: Beyond The Basics

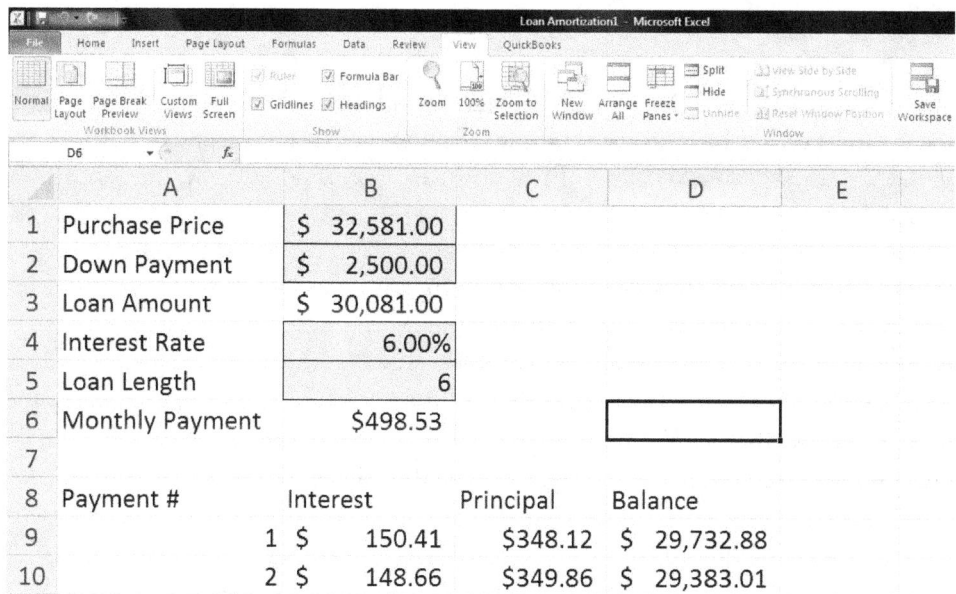

6. Enter the values as shown then click Save.

As when you used the Packing Slip template, Excel is forcing you to give this workbook a name. Saving the workbook will not affect the template. However, if you want to make changes to the template, you can simply make those changes and save the workbook as an Excel template. If you use the same name, Excel will overwrite the old template with the new one.

7. Close Excel.

Pat yourself on the back. You have survived Excel 2010: Beyond the Basics. Now, you just need to practice what you have learned and then apply it to your own Excel worksheets.

Index

Auto Outline 65
Charts
    Adding Data to 51
    Annotating 58
    Combining types 54
Comments 67
Data Validation 72
Freezing worksheet panes 76
Functions
    IF() 40
    PMT() 24
    SumIf() 42
    Vlookup() 34
Moving around 3
Named Ranges 35
Protection 69
transpose 78
Worksheets
    Grouping 17
    Inserting 9
    Linking 14, 16
    Protecting 69
    Renaming 9
    Transferring information between 10
    Ungrouping 19

Other books that may interest you

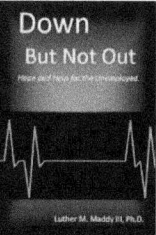
Down But Not Out: Hope and Help for the Unemployed
This book provides encouragement and practical advice for those dealing with a career transition of any kind, but especially unemployment. This book includes steps to maintain a positive attitude, resume tips, and advice on making the best interview impression possible. Online training and workbook also available.

Retail price: $12.95

Excel: The Basics (2013 or 2010)
In "learning by doing" you will gain a good grasp of the basics of Excel. You'll learn to create formulas, format and print worksheets, copy and move cell data, and generate attractive charts and graphs from your Excel data.

2013: Retail price: $9.95   2010: Retail price: $8.95

Excel: Beyond The Basics (2013 or 2010)
In "learning by doing" you will gain a good grasp of the Excel features beyond the basic level. You'll learn to create advanced formulas using Excel functions like PMT(), IF(), VLookup() and more. You'll also learn about worksheet protection, data validation, creating and using templates, advanced charting features, and much more.

Retail price: $9.95

Excel: Database and Statistical Features (2013 or 2010)
In "learning by doing" you will gain a good grasp of the Excel database features. You'll learn to create and use Pivot Tables and Charts. You'll also learn about database functions like DSum() and DAverage(). You'll also learn about filtering and subtotaling Excel data. Finally, you'll learn about performing statistical analysis using the Analysis Toolpak.

Retail price: $9.95

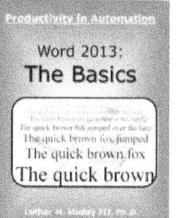
Word: The Basics (2013 or 2010)
In "learning by doing" you will learn the basics of MS Word. You'll also be introduced to performing tasks the most efficient way possible to increase your productivity. This workbook covers document creation and editing. You'll learn to copy and move and enhance text. You'll also learn about page a paragraph formatting, setting tabs, creating tables and more.

2013: Retail price: $9.95   2010: Retail price: $7.95

Word: Enhancing Documents (2013 or 2010)
In "learning by doing" you will learn the some of the desktop publishing features of Word. You'll learn to place text in columns, use Autoshapes, enhance mailing labels, and use and create styles. You'll also learn to add hyperlinks to your documents, how to use pre-defined templates, and much more.

2013: Retail price: $9.95   2010: Retail price: $8.95

Order wherever books are sold. Ordering in quantity?
Save 20% by ordering on our website: www.LutherMaddy.com

www.ingramcontent.com/pod-product-compliance
Lightning Source LLC
Chambersburg PA
CBHW081828170526
45167CB00007B/2752